TIME
OUT
for
MOMS

TIME OUT
for MOMS

Cheryl Woolsey Holloway

AUTUMN HOUSE® PUBLISHING COMPANY
P.O. Box 1139, Hagerstown, Maryland 21741-1139

Copyright © 1991 by
Autumn House® Publishing Company

The author assumes full responsibility for the accuracy of all facts and quotations as cited in this book.

This book was
Edited by James Cavil
Designed by Bill Kirstein
Cover Illustration by Joe Van Severen
Typeset: 11/12 Times Roman

Bible texts in this book are from *The New English Bible*. Copyright © The Delegates of the Oxford University Press and the Syndics of the Cambridge University Press 1961, 1970. Reprinted by permission.

PRINTED IN U.S.A.

96 95 94 93 92 91   10 9 8 7 6 5 4 3 2 1

Library of Congress Cataloging in Publication Data

Holloway, Cheryl Woolsey, 1956–
   Time out for moms / Cheryl Holloway.
      p.   cm.
   1. Mothers—Prayer-books and devotions—English. I. Title.
BV4847.B545 1991
242′ .6431—dc20
                                                        90-21992
                                                        CIP

ISBN 1-878951-06-8

Dedication

To my mother,
    who is still my best teacher
    in the art of mothering.

Foreword

Usually the lights are out in the nursery of our little country hospital. The lamb-print curtains hang forlornly in the window, and the pink and blue ribbon trim around the window droops. A nursery without a baby is a lonely place.

But just make a visit to the nursery window when a baby's arrival is around the corner! The lights flash on, the curtains swish back, and the window beams. A short, comfortably round woman bustles about with linens and baskets of supplies in blue and white disposable wrappers. She turns the heat lamp on a set of blankets, and readies the bath.

In a little while the new nursery occupant is dressed for the very first time. More than ready for a nap, the newborn is wrapped like a cocoon and placed in a bassinet before the bright nursery window for all the world to see.

I've participated rather distantly in the transformation of the nursery several times. I've never actually seen the lights turn on, being wrapped in my own cocoon of pain and activity. But when that is all over, my place is the room just across the hall from the nursery. The light from the nursery window drifts in through the partly open door. I can hear the patter of big and little feet down the hall and someone saying, "Let's see if there is a new baby in the nursery today."

I wait to hear the voices exclaim over the little stranger who is pretty much a stranger to me, too, except that she's mine. They say all the regular things like "Look at the tiny hands . . ." and "There's a pink card on the bassinet . . . ," and a child's voice pipes up, "It's making faces! Is it crying? Isn't anyone going to take care of it?"

I feel very warm and full of pride about my baby. Someone is taking care of her, but it's not me—I need a nap myself.

Marie Pelletier, the queen of the nursery, bustles the baby in to be nursed every so often. We both admire babies, she having raised hers already, and I with three or so back home. We're

7

pretty realistic about babies in general. We know about work and being tired and all that's coming up ahead.

Friends have brought carnations and sweet peas to set in my window, and the room is filling with fragrance. There is an old black-and-white film on the TV screen, and my doctor just dropped in to invite my husband and me to a private banquet. Just the two of us. Compliments of the hospital.

Mrs. Pelletier checks up on me again, and in her endearing French Canadian accent she confides that "babies are fun to take care of. But the most fun for me? I like to mother the mothers."

I feel like a girl again.

Most people will forget I'm a girl in the coming weeks and months. I probably will forget I was ever a girl myself, for a while at least. Babies have a way of demanding selfless motherhood. But to Mrs. Pelletier, I am just a girl. A girl who has had a baby, of course, but a girl like herself who has other loves besides the new baby and the family at home. Loves such as flowers and old romantic black-and-white movies, and a little time to herself where she can figure out who she is again.

The time is short. Mrs. Pelletier is reluctant to let me go. "I know it is expensive to stay in the hospital," she tells me. "But I wish all mothers could stay the entire three days. And longer. You need it," she says.

She's right. We do need this refreshing time with someone to share our responsibilities, to nurture us, to help us feel ourselves again! In these years when our children are so demanding—they really do need us, and we know it better than anyone—the less time we have to become reacquainted with life and ourselves, the more we need to get away for a while.

I hope these short devotions will help you do that. They'll help you stay in touch with God. His sustaining power is a resource mothers can't do without. And they'll help you feel that you are not alone. Other mothers carry the same burdens you do. Together we can gather, like the mothers and children before Jesus, and ask for His blessing.

As We Grow

Sarah can't talk much yet, but that doesn't stop her from holding forth with her doll. Most of the conversation consists of "um" and "hum" and mutterings under the breath close to the doll's head. Sarah adds plenty of soft pats and little kisses and tender glances. Sometimes she cocks her head to one side and nods with beguiling urgency as she points to some piece of doll furniture that she is trying to coax the doll into.

Sarah had to pick up these mother mannerisms from somewhere, and I assume they are mostly from me. I can't remember cocking my head to one side in order to coax anyone, but maybe I do. Sarah has been learning to be a mother every day of her short life. If she is anything like her 5-year-old sister, she will soon be wanting a real baby of her very own. I wouldn't be surprised if that dream will be with her most of her life!

My guess is that when she actually does have a baby, however, she will be very surprised about what it is like. The shock waves that will rock her lifestyle to its very roots are hard to comprehend—much less prepare for—beforehand.

New worries, new social pressures, new physical and emotional demands wreak havoc on all the habits and rhythms of the night and day that a woman has been accustomed to for most of her life. Suddenly she is not her own person anymore—she is a baby's mother.

But God has a special place in His heart for needy mothers. The Psalms are full of promises for us. Here's a cluster of them.

"Thou, Lord, dost make my lamp

burn bright.
and my God will lighten my darkness. . . .
He is the shield of all who take refuge
 in him.
What god is there but the Lord?
What rock but our God?—
The God who girds me with strength
and makes my way blameless,
who makes me swift as a hind
and sets me secure on the
 mountains'' (Psalm 18:28-33).

With God you can do more than just cope. You can have the serenity and strength that you need to leap up the mountain crags in your life as swiftly as a hind, and stand securely on the mountain peaks.

The Way
We Worry

Someone is crying, and my consciousness returns with a sickening lurch. I struggle out of bed, hurrying to quiet the baby so no one else in the house will wake up. You see, our floor squeaks. If someone else wakes up and has to use the bathroom, half the household might be padding around at 5:30 in the morning. At 5:30 the chances are slim of anyone getting back to sleep. The little ones will be cranky by midmorning, and take too early a nap—and be fussy all afternoon.

I wake up with every creak and bump in the night. If I get up to investigate the noise (and tell the child who made it to go back to bed), will my husband wake up? His 180 pounds on our floor will wake up the world.

I've braved winter gales in my nightgown because something was banging against the side of the house. I've oiled doors in houses that weren't mine. I've run the car in circles around the supermarket parking lot while my husband shops, in order to keep a baby in the back seat asleep. What we mothers won't do! We are a desperate lot.

Perhaps that's because our lives are tied so closely to those of our children. Every little frustration they suffer adds to our load of frustrations. Just watch a 2-year-old struggle to dress himself. He's screaming with frustration, but he screams louder when you try to help. You feel like screaming right along with him, don't you? It might as well be your coat and your fingers that are tied up in knots.

A mother's worries don't end when the children learn to sleep through the night or dress themselves. Many things torment a mother's heart as she stands back and watches her children tackle the perplexities of life.

Jeremiah knew all about frustration and worry. You can hear his agonized cries often in his writings. It wasn't any fun being worried over such a faithless people as Israel. Several times he wished he had never been born. Our frustrations are so very small beside Jeremiah's, but a worn mother's cry echoes in Jeremiah's lament: "Peace has gone out of my life. . . . Then I cry out that my strength has gone" (Lamentations 3:17, 18).

The chapter doesn't stop there, however. Next come some of the loveliest verses in the Bible.

"Therefore I will wait patiently:
the Lord's true love is surely not spent,
nor has his compassion failed;
they are new every morning,
so great is his constancy. . . .
It is good to wait in patience and sigh
for deliverance by the Lord" (verses 21-26).

11

Some of the most desperate prayers in my life have been for God to help the baby go to sleep—or stay asleep! God surely has bigger emergencies to care for. But He has an abundance of grace for mothers when they dangle at the end of their patience.

God's Kind of Comforting

Moo," Sarah calls excitedly. "Moo, moo, moo!" as our family drives past a herd of cattle. We all keep a sharp lookout for cows, horses, sheep, dogs, and, if we are lucky, a coyote or deer to show Sarah.

Today, however, things took a new twist. There were cattle just across the road from the house. We live in the middle of open range land, and though cattle aren't supposed to be on the highway, they often stray. Sarah had never seen cattle in that particular spot before. Suddenly she conceived the thought that cows might be something to worry about.

She couldn't go to sleep. "Moo," she cried in terror.

"The cows are gone," I said over and over. Her daddy went through each room calling, "Go *out!* Go *out,* cows! See, Sarah? No cows."

"Gone," Sarah repeated. "Out." But she still couldn't go to sleep.

At last I began to sing. I come to this point with every child. Long ago, when I was dreaming of the babies I was going to have, I memorized a number of beautiful old lullabies. Didn't every restless baby relax with a good lullaby?

But I discovered that lullabies didn't work with Baby No. 1. They didn't work with Nos. 2 or 3, either. All three of them hollered louder if I tried to sing when they were fussy. But I had to try a lullaby on Baby No. 4 anyway. And I sang her to sleep. I really did! It didn't take five full rounds of "Rock-a-bye Baby," her favorite lullaby (not mine).

God enjoys doing the same kind of nurturing and comforting that moms like to do. "It was I who taught Ephraim to walk," He reminisces, "I who had taken them in my arms; but they did not know that I harnessed them in leading-strings and led them with bonds of love—that I had lifted them like a little child to my cheek, that I had bent down to feed them" (Hosea 11:3, 4).

"As a mother comforts her son, so will I myself comfort you," He says in Isaiah 66:13. He wants to take care of whatever worries arise on our horizons. Most of them are no doubt as groundless as Sarah's worries about the cows, but He knows we lack perspective. He deals with us on our level. And since He's in a much better position than we are to take care of our problems, it makes sense to let Him.

> "Yet in my heart thou hast put more happiness
> than they enjoyed when there was corn
> and wine in plenty.
> Now I will lie down in peace and sleep;
> for thou alone, O Lord, makest me live unafraid"
> (Psalm 4:7, 8).

God's peace is a wonderful lullaby for the heart.

Rains of Righteousness

It doesn't take long for moms who are sitting around the edges of the cradle roll room to size up the cradle roll leader. We know she has a considerable amount of courage and self-confidence or she wouldn't be up front. And from the first moment that the children come in, her sense of humor begins to show. It's pretty hard to make it through a couple hours with a roomful of children without a bit of humor and poise.

Most interesting of all is watching the meeting of a woman's mind with a child's mind. That's one of the times when it seems that all the best in a woman shines forth. No one appreciates watching these kinds of talents more than a mother.

I can remember one particularly appealing woman who was the leader of the camp meeting cradle roll division. Her youngest was 5 or 6, which automatically put her in a more experienced bracket of motherhood than I. Her face glowed with the gentle graces of a saint, and she handled children in such a quiet, experienced way that I thought she might not reject the confidences of a young mother who was feeling pretty green.

We talked for quite a while. I told her that sometimes I felt like I had had too much of babies. I had only two then, but it seemed that I always had one on my back, or in my arms, or on my lap, or beside me in bed. If I wasn't feeding them, I was changing them, or washing them, or taking them in and out of the car.

"Did you ever," I asked her, "feel like you had handled or been handled by your children so much that you were used up and empty?"

"Times would come when I didn't want to be touched even

by my husband," she said. "I felt so overhandled that even a touch from him was painful."

When I heard that, I felt much better, knowing I wasn't alone in feeling these strange new burdens of motherhood. It must be that parched, used-up, empty feeling that makes Isaiah's cry come alive in a mother's heart.

"Rain righteousness, you heavens,
   let the skies above pour down;
   let the earth open to receive it,
   that it may bear the fruit of salvation
   with righteousness in blossom at its side"
(Isaiah 45:8).

Oh, to feel the heart-drenching rain of God's gracious patience and kindness! We are like farmers whose lands are cracked and dusty, running to stand with arms outstretched in a longed-for rain. We want God's goodness to pelt our faces and hearts till we are filled up with His love again.

Taking Time to Live Serenely

Maybe it was the scientist in me that made me sit back and watch. Angela, not yet 2, was trying to wrap her doll with a heavy baby-sized quilt. Her method was to drop the doll on the floor, throw the blanket on top of it, and then make sure all the loose ends were tucked up on top of the doll.

The blanket was so thick, however, that when she folded up the bottom corner the side corner fell open. She had to walk around the pile of blanket several times until every corner was in place—and then the blanket fell off the doll altogether.

By now Angela was complaining noisily to herself, but she replaced the blanket and tried to pick it up. The blanket quite filled her arms, and Angela walked off triumphantly, only to look back and see her doll still on the floor.

At last the mommy in me kicked into gear, and I helped her wrap up her doll, but my eyes were wet from laughter. Not that I didn't empathize with her! Often I too feel like I'm walking off with a lot of blanket and leaving the family behind. I put a lot of effort into things that I think should improve the quality of our home life, but I'm not so sure my programs always serve that purpose.

I wonder, for instance, whether some of the cooking I do that takes so much time and energy really helps the children in proportion to the effort I put into it. I had a chance to have lunch in the home of a young mother with five children. Her home was neat and organized, and yet she had just spent the morning home-schooling the three older ones. How had she managed to take care of her children and house and have company for lunch too?

I had brought along my four youngsters, and we all sat down at a table designed for a crew of harvesters. At her end of the table sat a huge casserole. My contribution to the meal was an enormous salad. That was our lunch! It was so delightfully simple.

Is your life more complicated than it needs to be? Stop for a few moments before you start your day. Relax, and repeat a few verses from the Psalms to get your viewpoint into perspective.

"The Lord is my shepherd; I shall want nothing.

He makes me lie down in green pastures,
and leads me beside the waters of peace;
he renews life within me" (Psalm 23:1-3).

"Let be then: learn that I am God,
high over the nations, high above earth"
(Psalm 46:10).

It's not a rat race God's asking you to live, is it? Take a good look at your day. Simplify it where you can. Clean up your daily work schedule like you clean clutter out of a closet—throw out what doesn't make your home life happier and better. Then, with your hand in God's, step into the day and live it serenely!

When Life Interrupts

Wの"hat did you do today?'' my husband will ask when he gets home tonight. He will look around as if the furniture ought to be dyed purple or some other major change should be obvious to account for all the time I've spent in the house.

I'd like to be able to point to a lot done. I have sewing projects and decorating projects and writing projects, not to mention a project so mundane as washing dishes, that I'd like to finish. But projects and children mix like oil and water. Take, for example, the following chronicle, the progression of one of my writing assignments I undertook when Sarah was a baby.

"Presently my 4-month-old is on my back, sucking her fingers. If she falls asleep, I can lay her down for a few moments of unhampered work time. I fire up the computer and start clearing the table, running back and forth between the table and computer, punching in commands and the return button, and wiping away crumbs. The 2-year-old awakens, and I assist her at the potty, and then she sits down with her older brother and sister playing with Legos in the living room.

"I am into my second paragraph. This is a good day! I put the sleeping baby down, and the 2-year-old joins me at the computer. In order to keep the baby asleep, I send the oldest two preschoolers outside into the subfreezing weather. Since it isn't windy, the toddler chooses to join them. The baby wakes up before I can get them all dressed and out the door.

"Huzzah! Paragraph three! The toddler is back in and on the potty again. So goes a mother's day."

No wonder we get despondent when we pick up a paper—particularly an alumni bulletin—and read about all the research and awards and *progress* going on in the rest of the world!

But do you think God looks at progress the same way we do? All the new advances in technology, the thousands of books being printed, the big business deals opened and closed in a day (while we put kids on and off the potty)—do you think all that impresses Him?

In a gloomy mood King Solomon wrote, "What has happened will happen again, and what has been done will be done again, and there is nothing new under the sun" (Ecclesiastes 1:9). He too wanted what he did to matter in the long run, but he discovered that what he felt was important wasn't what God thought was important.

> "I have seen the business that God
> has given men to keep them busy.
> He has made everything to suit its
> time. . . .
> I know that there is nothing good
> for man except to be happy and
> live the best life he can while
> he is alive.
> Moreover, that a man should eat
> and drink and enjoy himself, in
> return for all his labours, is a
> gift of God.
> I know that whatever God does lasts
> for ever; to add to it or subtract
> from it is impossible"
> (Ecclesiastes 3:10-14).

The Shaker hymn puts it this way: " 'Tis a gift to be simple, 'tis a gift to be free, 'tis a gift to come down to where you ought to be." The gift of life is for each moment, for finding happiness in each small daily duty. Mothers whose hands are filled with nurturing duties for their small charges have their fingers on the very pulse of life and progress.

Why We Get Angry

My husband leaned on one elbow in bed and stared at me for such a long time that I asked what he was doing. "I'm trying to figure out how much of you is still the girl I married," he said.

This promised to be an interesting revelation. "How am I different?" I asked.

"You are more mature," he said. "And angrier."

When I repeated this conversation in one of my classes, one of my students, a young Navajo mother of four, nodded her head.

"My husband says I'm mean now," she said. "He tells me I was nice when he met me. But now when he gets home I just blow up at him. He comes home so happy to see the children. But I've been running around all day taking care of them and cleaning the house and cooking, and when he comes home I just sit down and blow up at him."

What makes angry mothers? Is it all the work we have to do? Is it lack of appreciation? Is it our low status in society? Our chronic fatigue? A mother's working conditions often contain irritating circumstances, but I believe we can be buoyant enough to rise above them. We can make adjustments in our attitudes and habits that can help us cope with many of the tensions of motherhood.

I am beginning to see (sometimes too late to save the situation, but late is better than never) that my unrealistic expectations often set me up for stress and anger. For instance, I expect to have all the house clean at one time, preferably sometime between 4:00 and 6:00 on Friday afternoons. This may sound like a joke, but it's important to me, and I haven't managed it yet.

I expect our kids to sleep at night, and not have to go to the bathroom in the morning until everybody in the house is ready to wake up. I expect them to absorb some of the finer aspects of civilization rather than expecting me to teach them every last detail, such as why they should pick up what they drop.

But however reasonable these and other expectations that mothers have seem to be, they rarely match what really happens, and so we get angry. What we need to do instead is change (or postpone) our expectations. Since most of us have never been in charge of a houseful of kids before, we have to feel our way to a realistic understanding of how a house with normal kids in it looks, and how normal kids—and moms—behave.

One Sabbath a courageous mother invited a houseful of company, including our family, home for dinner after church. Part of her preparations for the meal included wiping down the kitchen chairs. It was the loveliest thing she could have done! I saw that it was normal for mothers of small children to worry about their company sitting on sticky seats! All the spilled food at our house became a little less threatening to my concept of a normal household.

Once Jesus said something very comforting, and I like to think that His compassionate eyes dwelt especially long on the mothers in the crowd as He said it.

"Come to me, all whose work is
hard, whose load is heavy; and I
will give you relief. Bend your
necks to my yoke, and learn from
me, for I am gentle and humble-

20

hearted, and your souls will find
relief. For my yoke is good to
bear, my load is light''
(Matthew 11:28-30).

Our unrealistic expectations (and sometimes those we feel others have for us) are whips that drive us to desperate acts. But who wants to be remembered as an angry mom? Jesus says *His* yoke is good to bear, and His load is light. What a relief for ourselves and our families when we drop the load we find so difficult to carry, and pick up His!

Crashing the
Pity Party

Households with children are notorious for the large number of disasters they sustain during a day. Moms tend to get somewhat acclimated to crises, but still things happen that knock us off our even keel.

Once Heather, 2, was trying to get up into her chair at the table. She fell off, accompanied by bangs and crashes from a variety of items that had been on the table. She set up a fearsome howl, and I dashed into the dining room from the bedroom, where I was nursing the baby.

As I was picking up the pieces around the table, Joshua fell off his ride-on truck with all the screams necessary to bring the world running. I turned to bring him to order just as the baby fell off the bed.

There's nothing like all the children crying at once to put a cutting edge on nerves. Unless it's walking into the kitchen to see them swimming in a half gallon of salad oil spilled on the floor.

Or finding all the leftovers from the refrigerator being stirred into the bathwater. Each mother has her own set of horror stories, but we all know the feeling of "Aaaaaacck! I don't want to look. I don't want to be here. I wish I were in China!"

Our horror stories may sound funny five months down the road, but at the time they take an enormous amount of emotional energy. Mothers who are already stressed with fatigue, isolation, and feelings of futility have a hard time being patient and composed during a crisis.

Self-pity often complicates the picture. Our isolation tends to make us turn inward, and we find ourselves counting up all the ills that have accumulated during the days and weeks. We finger them mentally over and over, wondering how we came to deserve such misery. Self-pity saps us of any reserves of composure and self-control we might have had, and everyday crises can turn us into ugly things.

The psalm writer, master as he was at describing human emotion, describes self-pity, too.

> "So it was all in vain that I kept
> my heart pure and washed my hands
> in innocence.
> For all day long I suffer torment
> and am punished every morning.
> *Yet had I let myself talk on in this*
> *fashion. I should have betrayed the*
> *family of God.*"

It's human to feel sorry for all the awful things that happen to us. But it is dangerous! We cannot indulge in it. What can we do? The psalmist writes on.

> "So I set myself to think this out
> but I found it too hard for me,
> until I went into God's sacred courts;
> there I saw clearly what their end would be"
> (Psalm 73:13-17).

Our trials can't overwhelm us when they are placed in the

context of God's overall plan. We see that these times will pass. The gummy, indescribable messes we plunge our hands into in the name of housekeeping will come to an end. Thoughtlessness, impatience, drudgery, exhaustion, hatred, and all the curses of this old life will be gone.

God has a new and better world coming. And the good news is that as we see life through God's perspective, it begins even now!

Each One Different

Despite the millions of babies this old world has seen, each new baby is different. You would think that after all the thousands of years of babies being born and growing up, it ought to be pretty easy to find out how to put a baby to sleep for a reasonable length of time, and how to feed one, and what to do when it throws a tantrum because you can't understand what it's trying to say.

But with each new baby the same questions pop up all over again. Moms the world over go through the same trial and error process of finding out how their own new piece of babyhood seems to flourish the best.

It's at night when the baby is screaming instead of sleeping that I have my biggest doubts about the proper steps for mothering. That's when I wish most for some sort of manual detailing how to handle the particular model malfunctioning in its little bed. How many times should I get up and try to do something? If I let it cry, will it feel abandoned and psychologically abused for the rest of its life? Will Dave's firm, masculine voice do the trick, or will he make the baby hysterical?

Something good comes from these struggles to understand and deal with each of our children, however. If children were like houseplants that need water only once a week to thrive, how well would we come to know them? How closely would our lives become tied to theirs?

There is so little we actually understand about the development of our children, though it takes place under our very noses! How much less we would understand of their complexity and individuality if we didn't *have* to become involved in the very intricate processes of their lives. Giving children so much hands-on care is good for our long-term relationships with them. But it's also a cause of much of the stress young moms feel.

Fortunately for our children and for us, however, God is good at being intimate. He is very attentive to our individual patterns, to our developmental quirks, to everything that makes us unique.

"Lord, thou hast examined me and knowest me.
Thou knowest all, whether I sit down or rise up;
thou hast discerned my thoughts from afar.
Thou hast traced my journey and my resting
places,
and art familiar with all my paths.
For there is not a word on my tongue
but thou, Lord, knowest them all.
Thou hast kept close guard before me and behind
and hast spread thy hand over me"
(Psalm 139:1-5).

It's nice to know that despite all the people in the world, God knows about every little idiosyncrasy we have. He knows why we feel the way we do. He knows what we need, even when we don't. He also knows what our children need when we don't.

In fact, God knows every individual in the world so well that we can trust Him with every intimate aspect of our lives and our children's lives. Everything God has ever said or done adds proof

24

upon proof that we can trust Him. He will not fail us. He cannot fail us, for He is God.

About Paper Plates, Mops, and Other Exciting Things

Sometimes I can be really efficient at cleaning the house. A few minutes ago I cleared the dirty paper plates from the table, leaving a clean stack of plates at each place setting. That took care of doing the dishes and setting the table for the next meal, and I'll use the dirty paper plates for starting the fire tonight.

I'll let you in on a couple other housekeeping tips, too. I've been years developing these. Need something to take care of the mineral deposits in the baby's potty because it sat full overnight? Fill the potty with water and add a little LimeAway. Soak a few minutes and clean. If you rub soap on the bottom and sides of the potty, it will be easier to clean next time.

That about exhausts my repertoire of tips for making housekeeping easy. Most of the time I go about things the hard way. I let the food dry hard as a rock on the dishes before I wash them. (That's why I like to use paper plates.) I put the toddler's Sabbath dress on before breakfast rather than after. I even let the children play in the bathroom.

The reason I do things the hard way is that I'm trying very hard to make things easy on myself. Have you ever tried to get a toddler to eat when she's excited and wants to get dressed in her Sabbath clothes like everyone else? Three bites and she's full.

She refuses another morsel. You get the dress on, and in a few minutes there she is at your elbow, begging for a bite of *your* breakfast. You haven't time to undress her and put her, screaming, back into her chair, so you feed her, spilling food on both your outfits.

That's why I dress her, feed her, and hose her down before we go to church. It's easier that way.

The reason I let the kids play in the bathroom is that I don't have a water table for water play like child-care centers have. I have to make do, and the easiest way to manage in the winter—our usual weather in Montana—is to let the kids play at the sink.

I look at the bright side of the picture. When the playing is done and the kids have changed their clothes, they will be clean. They will be happily enriched with the educational experience of water play. Besides that, the floor will be freshly mopped with all the water that was spilled on it!

I guess what I'm trying to say is that the longer I struggle with this business of keeping the house and kids clean, the easier it is to take housekeeping—and messes—less seriously. There's more than one side to every mess, and we might as well look at the brightest side! There's more than one way to do any job, and we might as well figure out the easiest, least stressful way to do it.

Part of the job of eliminating stress in keeping house is figuring out priorities. Deciding what it is *you* feel must be done in order to survive in the house. Your list may be far different from your neighbor's, but your neighbor isn't going to live in your house.

One of my top priorities is keeping the living room picked up. The bedroom may be piled high with unfolded laundry and the sink may be full of dishes, but if I can see the couch cushions and the floor, I feel like life hasn't gotten totally out of control.

I need to feel in control of the house in order to feel good about myself. But I recognize that because of the career choices I've made, some housekeeping jobs can't get done as often as I'd like. Since I've asked God to guide me in each daily decision, career and otherwise, and I believe I'm doing His will, I've come to the conclusion that I don't need to feel guilty for those things I simply can't do in a day.

I've learned to ask God to help me find time for undone tasks that are really bothering me, and to bother me about the things I ought to be doing but don't feel a burden for. After I do what I believe God thinks I ought to do, why worry about the rest?

Paul puts it beautifully.

> "The Lord is near; have no anxiety, but in everything
> make your requests known to God in prayer and petition
> with thanksgiving. Then the peace of God, which is
> beyond our utmost understanding, will keep guard over
> your hearts and your thoughts, in Christ Jesus"
> (Philippians 4:6).

God is good at taking stress out of our lives! We labor under so many concerns and frustrations that He never intended for us to worry about. If God keeps house with us, we can learn to see past our little house worries into His great dwelling place, where contentment is always at home.

Contentment

In our world where bigger and better is so much before us on TV, in the neighbor's house, and on every magazine cover, contentment is a rare art. Young families struggling to reach a solid financial footing find it especially hard to remember what contentment is. There is, after all, so much we don't have, and worries of bills that need to be paid. How rarely we have money even for a baby-sitter.

As if financial worries weren't enough, there are problems

with having a family that we never dreamed of as girls. Whoever thought that having kids could be such a 30-hour-a-day worry? We worry about babies choking on the Legos or falling into the toilet headfirst or having enough blankets on but not too many blankets on. Then the babies grow, and we have to referee fights between kids, marshal the toy explosion all over the house, and keep everyone in matching socks and shoes.

We feel tied to the house. Tied to the children. The days are gone when we could just up and go when we felt like it. We can't even take a shower or a nap without hearing the house fall apart as soon as the door shuts behind us.

Sometimes we wonder whatever happened to the days when we wanted these children, anyway. Then we give a guilty start, half glancing around to see if anyone heard us think that awful thought. But there it stands, bold and bad, the awful feeling that motherhood isn't what it's cracked up to be, and it lasts forever. I remember one mother admitting that she kept M&M's hidden in her apron pocket. She said that she sneaked one every once in a while, just to keep her courage up!

Can we as young mothers who are isolated, busy, sometimes irritated, and often tired still be contented with our lot? Contentment is often assumed to be a feeling. We believe that we are content when we feel happy with the way everything is going in our life. But if we have to wait on our feelings for happiness and contentment, we may wait forever. Feelings are too flighty to depend on.

Instead, we mothers can *decide* to be content. We can *decide* to be happy with what we have in life. Rather than worrying about what we don't have, we can rejoice over what we do have that is good. The writers of the Psalms point out the best foundation for contentment.

"Whom have I in heaven but thee?
And having thee, I desire nothing else on earth.
Though heart and body fail,
yet God is my possession for ever" (Psalm 73:25,26).

28

"Thou, Lord, my allotted portion, thou my cup,
thou dost enlarge my boundaries:
the lines fall for me in pleasant places,
indeed I am well content with my inheritance"
(Psalm 16:5, 6).

When God is the portion that belongs to us, and He is so much more than everything we could dream of, how can we help being content? Finances may come and finances may go. Since it's God we are depending on rather than finances, we can be content.

Families are hard work, no doubt about it. But if we had no families, wouldn't our lives have much less meaning? God has enlarged our boundaries, and in doing so, He has made it possible for us to experience more contentment and happiness than we ever dreamed!

God's Darling

As I opened the refrigerator I happened to glance at Sarah, still in her high chair at the breakfast table. She was staring across her oatmeal with that curious gaze of someone who isn't seeing what she is looking at. Something about the rhythms in "The Drummer Boy" playing on the stereo had absorbed her attention. She was nodding and swaying her little head as if she had never heard anything like it before.

She probably hadn't heard anything like it, though we play lots of music at our house. It wasn't the music that was different—it was something inside of her that was newly awakened to something she was hearing. I love music too, and I stood at the fridge watching her as long as the enchantment of the music held her, happy just to be able to look on.

On another day Josh, who was 7 at the time, leaped up from where he had been sitting on the carpet listening to Uncle Dan and Aunt Sue's *Story Hour* tapes. His eyes were sparkling with discovery. "Mom," he said, "guess what! I just figured something out! Booker T. Washington and the Wright brothers must be in the same family, because they both have a sister named Ruby!"

Oh, the joy of logic! It makes the puzzle pieces of the world come together like magic. Josh's facts weren't all straight, but that wonderful process of finding patterns of meaning in what seem at first random facts had demonstrated its potential with a dazzle that thrilled him.

I had found, when Josh was 6, that I couldn't skip over dates as I generally feel like doing when we read about Lincoln's life and the building of the Golden Gate bridge and things like that. Dates mean nothing to me, and I didn't think they would interest a 6-year-old. But for Josh they have a strange significance. He pounces on them like a cat on a mouse, playing with them, comparing them to other events in our reading.

"Why, Mom," he exclaimed when we read that the first barrages on the Nile had been completed in 1890. "This is 1990. That was 100 years ago!" Whatever titillated him about the coincidence in dates escaped me. I was thrilled with his excitement, however, for I know what it is to experience the serendipity of discovery. He finds it in history's dates! How odd! How wonderful!

Wisdom is a delightful thing. Personified, she describes herself in Proverbs 8. "The Lord created me the beginning of his works, before all else that he made, long ago," she says (verse 22). "When He set the heavens in their place I was there, when he girdled the ocean with the horizon, when he fixed the canopy of clouds overhead" (verses 27, 28).

> "Then I was at his side each day,
>   his darling and delight,
>   playing in his presence continually,

playing on the earth, when he had finished it,
while my delight was in mankind. . . .
For he who finds me finds life
and wins favour with the Lord'' (verses 30-35).

Mothers have a ringside seat as they watch the blossoming interest and pleasure of their children as they learn wisdom. It's one of the joys of motherhood, one of the things that makes our work worthwhile. How good of God to share His darling, His delight, His plaything Wisdom with our children and with us! And what a shame it would be if we become so busy with housekeeping and child-tending that we miss the delight of her presence.

Learning to Wait

Sarah insists on getting into her crib by herself. It is usually the wisest thing to let her do it; if I put her in, I will have to spend the next 15 minutes explaining to a very upset youngster why Mommy thought it best to save time.

So I stand in the doorway and watch Sarah study the crib. She looks down at the bottom rail and fingers the side ones. She turns around and smiles up at me. Tentatively she steps up onto the bottom rail and bounces a little. She glances around the room and stretches her neck to see past the crib headboard and out the window.

Then she tests the next step, the mattress. Carefully she slides her leg across the top rail and straddles it in meditation for some minutes. At last she lets herself slide down onto the bed and grins up at me. "Potty," she says.

Toddlers enjoy stretching an experience to its limits. The trouble is that our patience gets stretched to its limits too.

It's all the time that goes into the little things over and over again that mothers often find difficult to have patience for. We have so many things to do that we feel time whistling by our ears while we stand by watching a child go through all the rituals of growing up. And we have to stand by and watch, because we're needed.

We have to watch a fastidious youngster carefully tear off a square of tissue paper and fold it five times before using it. We must wait while she goes through three squares of tissue paper this way, because she wanted to use the "big potty" and we don't want her to fall in.

We have to help her pull her dolly's pants down so it can use the potty too—and we must wait a respectable length of time as it sits there, and have a tissue ready for the little mommy to use at the proper moment. Then there's the matter of washing and drying hands—all done with due ceremony. This following of rituals and teaching of rituals takes lots and lots of time and forbearance.

After living with several toddlers, however, I find that I've loosened up on the last one to come through the family ranks. It's easier to understand why all the time is needed. It's easier to have the patience to stand by and watch the baby learn to grow up. Maybe it's because I've finally realized that nothing I can do will help her learn any faster! And as I ponder her development, I realize she doesn't need to learn any faster. She's doing fine just the way she is, and I'm learning to slow down and enjoy her experiences with her as she tastes life.

Sometimes we try to go through life too fast even for God. Have you ever counted the "wait for the Lord" phrases in the Psalms? You might enjoy doing it as part of your devotions some time. There's something about the experience of waiting for God to act on our behalf that is good for us.

"Commit your life to the Lord;
trust in him and he will act.
He will make your righteousness

shine clear as the day and the justice
of your cause like the sun at noon.
Wait quietly for the Lord,
be patient until he comes;
do not strive to outdo the successful
nor envy him who gains his ends''
(Psalm 37:5-7).

After all, if we are in too big of a hurry for the children, and too big of a hurry for God, we are really leaving all that's important behind!

Being Fussy

The girls have set up a bed in the living room made of two dining room chairs placed face-to-face. Heather, 6, is the "baby," and Sarah, 2, is the "mommy." Heather has opted to be a very fussy baby, but she lets Sarah comfort and quiet her, and then Sarah dramatically tiptoes away.

As Sarah reaches halfway across the room, Heather drops her doll and begins fussing again. Sarah quickens her pace to the other side of the room, where she sighs loudly, but remains while the fussing continues for a moment or two. Eventually she returns, and the cycle repeats itself.

It looks suspiciously like the very thing Sarah and I enact at bedtime. I wonder at Sarah's astuteness. How does she know how carefully I walk away from her room so as to not emphasize the fact that I am leaving? Perhaps she can hear the difference between my bedtime walk and my rest-of-the-time walk. But when she begins fussing, how can she tell that I abandon the tiptoe walk and proceed at a normal pace to my chair, where I sigh and rest before I answer the summons again?

And there's this matter of the calculated wait before mommy answers the fussing. We are both familiar with the bedtime fussing routine. It's a ritual we go through often enough to know our parts very well. Sarah has the "I want water" fuss, and the "my blanket isn't covering my feet" fuss, the "sing to me" one, the "I dropped something" one, and of course, the "I don't know what I want, but I can't settle down" one.

It's during the last fuss that I wait before coming back into the bedroom, hoping that during a long delay baby will get tired of complaining and drop off to sleep.

The relationship between a mother and child is complex. Research shows that mothers who try to keep their babies' needs answered are rewarded with babies who eventually become less fussy. Mothers who do not consistently try to keep their little ones happy (often so as not to "spoil" them) find their children are still fussy later in life.

Culture, personality, and the individual requirements of each relationship all have a bearing on how mothers encourage their little ones to grow up. But most mothers, even the most attentive, eventually try to help their little ones learn some measure of independence.

This whole dilemma sounds curiously like the complaints in a number of psalms. Take for example, the following one.

> "How long, O Lord, wilt thou quite forget me?
> How long wilt thou hide thy face from me?
> How long must I suffer anguish in my soul,
>   grief in my heart, day and night?
> How long shall my enemy lord it over me?
> Look now and answer me, O Lord my God. . . .
> But for my part I trust in thy true love.
> My heart shall rejoice, for thou hast set me
>   free.
> I will sing to the Lord, who has granted me
>   all my desire" (Psalm 13:1-6).

A rather fussy prayer, when you think about it. Quite a few

of ours are! Yet this one was recorded in the Holy Book by an understanding God.

God doesn't always answer our pleas as quickly as we'd like Him to, though He could in a twinkle. But He still declares that He is loving. Have you ever wondered why? Perhaps it's because immediately helping us out of every little crisis we get into wouldn't help us in the long run.

God wants us to see our problems in the same perspective He does. Once we see our troubles as very small in the light of His ultimate goodness to us, we can rest in perfect peace—whatever happens. We know we have an attentive Father who, in His own good time, will grant our every desire. And because we are very sure of His goodness to us, we can sing now!

On Being a Picturebook Mother

Before I was married, I bought a beautiful book about mothers from Hallmark. It has soft pictures of mothers with babies in their arms, and poems that start off like this one: "I saw a young mother . . . with eyes full of laughter . . . and two little shadows . . . came following after." I haven't read it much since my first baby came along. Sometimes I wonder if motherhood will ever seem romantic again.

The last scratched knee that a good mother would have kissed was accompanied with loud screams while I was taking an important phone call. Mothers in books enjoy dressing up their little girls' hair with ribbons. I need to hire someone just to keep my children's hair brushed.

I usually don't feel like the picturebook ideal of a mother who has soft hands and a clean white apron, who arranges flowers and never lets the baking burn while she keeps the house and everybody in it neat and clean and up to snuff. But sometimes I do! Christmas transforms me into a housewife and mother of rare caliber. For me, anyway.

I love to clean house at Christmas. I dust the chandelier and wash windows and clear off the mantle so I can hang up garlands and crocheted snowflakes and set up the candles. I love to cook at Christmas. The children and I cut out our sugar cookies and gingerbread girls and boys, frosting and decorating them, and I bake fancy breads and cook up custard for creamy, homemade eggnog.

I enjoy supervising the children in making our Christmas tree into the most magic of trees. For the final touch I arrange a porcelain and lace angel on the topmost branch. One of the gold tree lights illuminates her soft face as she presides over the toy-laden tree. Queen of the Christmas romance lit up about her, she watches over the children curled in their sleeping bags around the tree on Christmas Eve. She looks and looks, like me, and never tires of looking.

How easy it is to be a mother sometimes. But then there are all those other times when we don't feel like proper mothers at all. It's not always easy to understand ourselves and why we feel the way we do.

The many facets of our natures have needs and expectations that we have various degrees of success in fulfilling. When the house is looking good and the kids are happy, we may feel great about how good we are as moms. Other times, our unrealistic expectations and lack of skills create a no-win situation, and we feel guilty, frustrated, and discontented.

The ebb and flow of hormones in our bodies also affect the way we feel about ourselves. We may begin the month's cycle feeling the optimism and energy of a supermom but finish the month out as the Wicked Witch of the West. In the ups and downs, ins and outs of our emotional selves, God's promises are wonderful anchors of constancy.

> "Blessed be the Lord,
> for he has heard my cry for mercy.
> The Lord is my strength, my shield,
> in him my heart trusts;
> so I am sustained, and my heart
> leaps for joy,
> and I praise him with my whole body"
> (Psalm 28:6, 7).

We know God created the sea, with its changeful temperament under lashing gales, warm winds, and calm; just so He created women, with our vast capacity for emotional reactions. We know "the Lord on high is mightier far than the noise of great waters" (Psalm 93:4), and He is our Master, too. We can trust Him as Pilot and Guide as we learn to understand and regulate our emotional natures.

Ups and Downs

When I was 19, I made the following entry in my diary. "Oh, I would hold out my arms to the world and embrace the sky and wind and fly and sing and dance and fling around. I can't tear myself away from outside. It is very exciting to be alive! O God! I know my emotions can't take this emotional high for long—but don't let me drop into emotional depths later, just to balance the way I feel now. Help me, please!"

I'd lived long enough to be scared of my own emotional upheavals. Even in the midst of euphoria, I remembered the depression with which my body paid for any overblown flights of elation.

Those who have studied the chemical balances in the brain can explain how the buildup of one chemical connected with euphoria produces an opposite chemical reaction designed to depress emotions and produce equilibrium. Other chemicals affect our emotions too.

Many women take the Pill with no changes in their disposition, but when I was on the Pill, my emotions went dead. Nothing seemed interesting, good, or enjoyable. A few days after I quit taking the drug, a silly little thought bubbling through my head made me laugh out loud. Suddenly I realized how impossible it would have been for that simple thought to make me laugh a few days earlier. What I had always considered a naturally happy, permanent part of my personality had been affected by a tiny bit of hormone.

Jean Lush, in her book *Emotional Phases of a Woman's Life,* describes the effects of our monthly cycle on our emotions. She shows how our emotions range from confidence and exuberance at the beginning of the month, to moodiness in the middle of the month, and irritability, depression, and hostility at the end of the cycle.

As a small child I can remember the power my mother had over the emotional climate in our home. I can remember waking up and wondering if the day was going to be a happy day or a mad one! We mothers make the weather in the home. When we are sunny, the whole household is warmed and contented. When we cloud over, a gray pall falls over the rest of the family.

I determined as a child to keep a happy temperament in my home, but it's amazing how much easier that is to say than do. Sometimes I am a warm, winsome, good-as-gold mother. And sometimes, to my horror and the children's bewilderment, I'm a harassed, frizzy-haired, get-out-of-the-kitchen-NOW ogre.

Lush suggests planning for the times when it seems so impossible to respond properly to frustrations. Try to plan to do difficult jobs when you know you'll be more up to it. Hire a baby-sitter and get away for a while. One desperate young mother, about to lose control of her emotions and terrified she would hurt the children, locked herself in her bedroom and called her husband at work to take over during the emergency.

Chemistry has an important role in our emotional lives, but we don't have to be a slave to chemistry. Peter talks about an invaluable, *lasting* commodity women can possess, if they would value it.

> "Your beauty should reside, not in outward
> adornment—the braiding of the hair, or
> jewellery, or dress—but in the inmost
> centre of your being, with its imperishable
> ornament, a gentle, quiet spirit, which is
> of high value in the sight of God"
> (1 Peter 3:3, 4).

James tells us where we can get it.

> "Make no mistake, my friends. All good giving,
> every perfect gift, comes from above, from the
> Father of the lights of heaven. With him there
> is no variation, no play of passing shadows"
> (James 1:17).

Our bright, energetic, ebullient feelings are a gift from God, and we can thank Him for them. When the bright part of our nature fails us, God, who made us and understands the frailty of our emotions, can keep us constant, stable, capable of coping with our emotions on the one hand and our family's needs on the other.

But through all our emotional phases, the high ones and the low ones, we can have at the center of our lives a gentle and quiet spirit. A spirit that seeks God's grace in good times for direction and sensitivity, and depends on God's grace in bad times for strength, stability, and peace.

Self

On my way home after teaching class a few days ago, I stopped at a convenience store for a magazine. As I was searching the shelves, I came across a women's slick called *Self*. *How like our wicked generation,* I thought, *to spawn a magazine called* Self; and behaving as a proper Christian, I turned to such decent titles as *Family Circle* and *Better Homes and Gardens*.

After scanning my options, however, most of the articles I wanted to read (they appeared to be perfectly healthy and reputable) happened to be in *Self*. So I took that magazine with its blazing title up to the cashier and paid for it before God and everybody.

Facing me at home were many duties—mainly the children. Four of them. It still astonishes me sometimes that I have four children—I find myself counting them every once in a while, just to be sure. Their number never seems more overwhelming than when they all greet me at the door—"Mommy, Mommy, Mommy, *Mommy!*"—as if they can't really believe I'm finally home. I look into each of their eager faces and feel the intensity of the bonds that attach us to each other.

Remembering the children, I drove home slowly, looking at the mountains. We live in the foothills of the Rockies, and I never tire of looking at them. I glanced across the car seat at my new magazine. If I were self-*less,* I thought, I would be driving faster. I was needed at home. But I needed the mountains. I needed a few minutes of quiet thought before I moved from meeting my students' needs to meeting my family's needs.

Thinking about dealing with my own needs makes me quite as uncomfortable as buying a magazine called *Self*. I know that taking time for myself means taking less time for others. In that light, self seems like incredibly selfish baggage.

But is it really? Is self bad? In theology, self is usually the enemy because it often takes precedence over God and others. And yes, I would say that self is bad.

In my Early Childhood classes, however, I emphasize the importance of helping children develop *self-esteem*. Self-esteem is the foundation of every healthy relationship in life. Children who believe themselves as basically unworthy of love and attention grow up to have difficulties in their work and their relationship with a boss, and are never really secure in an intimate relationship.

If children are surrounded with love and acceptance till they are fairly saturated with security, however, they will be able to love and accept others. They have to be filled in order to give. And moms do too!

Think of a beautiful mountain lake that feeds a busy stream running down through the valley. If the lake just fed the stream, it would soon be empty. But the lake is constantly being fed itself by countless streamlets and cataracts from the mountains round about. It's a law of life that in order to give, you must receive.

A mother's needs for rest and peace, for security and love, for mental stimulation and development, are human and normal. Mothers who have ignored their own needs have a difficult time when their family grows up. Suddenly they realize they are just an empty shell, that their reason for living—taking care of the children—no longer exists. Other women become so angry at being deprived that they strike out at their family and society, blaming others for the emptiness and stress in their lives.

A wise woman recognizes that she does have needs, and that she cannot always depend on her mate or family or friends to meet them. But she also knows who is responsible for caring for her needs.

> "Unless the Lord builds the house,
>   its builders will have toiled in vain.
> Unless the Lord keeps watch over a city,
>   in vain the watchman stands on guard.

41

In vain you rise up early and go late to rest,
   toiling for the bread you eat;
   he supplies the need of those he loves''
(Psalm 127:1, 2).

A happy woman understands her own humanity, but also understands the compassion and strength of the God who undergirds her life. We don't have to be superwomen, being all things to all people at the expense of ourselves; we have a super God, who is all things to all people, including ourselves!

In simple faith we can accept His gifts of rest in due season, the healing power of music, the strength that comes from friendships, the soul food found in a walk. We can take these gifts with joy and not guilt, in the same way that we accept God's love. We know that it is His design that our lives be filled with the contentment and strength that His goodness brings.

Time to Be Alone

I sprawled across an easy chair and stared at the ceiling one night after all the children were asleep. "If you're as tired as you say you are," my husband asked, "why don't you go to bed?"

"Because then I won't know that I'm alone," I said. "I'll fall asleep, and it will be morning, and there will be the children again. I want to feel alone for a little while!"

We mothers do all kinds of things to find a little privacy and peace. One trick is to send Daddy into the early-morning racket outside the bedroom door, and hide with a pillow over your head. Another one is to retreat into the bathroom and lock the door.

Part-time work and hobbies are helpful in keeping your own sense of identity strong. Some mothers are happy to stay home with the children, and feel completely fulfilled taking care of cooking and canning, gardening, home decorating, and all the creative aspects of child rearing. Others find they need some interest outside the home to keep them fresh and motivated inside the home. They feel like they need to make some "contribution to society"—though they recognize the importance of their task of rearing children.

I'm happy for the mothers who are content at home, but I find myself in the second category. After a couple hours of part-time teaching at a community college, I can come home and really see my children when I look at them. I feel fresh and ready to tackle my family responsibilities again.

Another thing you can do to keep your feeling of self intact is to pick a part of the day that is just yours. It might be when your husband gets home and you can take a shower at last. It might be after all the children are in bed and you can sit down.

Do whatever you feel like doing during your special time. Read. Listen to the stereo. Take a walk. Soak in a scented bath. Don't clean the house or fold clothes. Make your time a mini-vacation that you can count on every day, even if it's only for 15 or 20 minutes.

Eventually you can pick up many of the habits and patterns that gave your life security and purpose before the children came along. Your life won't be turned inside out forever. But to make these transitions easier, don't forget to hold God to His promise of directing each part of your day. You can count on His reassurances; His word is never false.

> "I have set the Lord continually before me:
> with him at my right hand I cannot be shaken.
> . . .Thou wilt show me the path of life;
> in thy presence is the fullness of joy,
> in thy right hand pleasures for evermore"
> (Ps 16:8-11).

Feeling Good
About Ourselves

I turned quickly away from the mirror over the sink. I had learned to ignore mirrors in general, but sometimes I forgot. The woman I had just seen didn't appeal to me at all, but there wasn't much I was prepared to do about it.

After Joshua was born, time seemed to evaporate like steam erupting from an hysterical kettle. I had neither the time nor energy to put in contact lenses, take them out, and cleanse them. I went back to wearing my old eyeglasses. The red-tinted frames brought out all the red splotches in my face, and the plastic lenses were scratched. I looked out at life through a white haze, but at least I could tell the baby from the blankets.

Perhaps some of the hardest hit parts of a new mother's lifestyle are the things she has been doing for herself. Wellness programs, reading, quiet times with her husband and with God, and other efforts at self-improvement and relaxation are often crowded out with the demands children place on a mother's time.

The things that we do for ourselves seem to be the easiest to drop. Without them, a mother's self-esteem plummets. But you can introduce a few simple activities into your daily schedule that will build up your self-esteem and inner strength.

Try making your mirror your friend instead of your enemy. Smile at yourself every time you pass one. Make some encouraging comment out loud, such as "You did a beautiful job cleaning up the sink" or "Those colors sure look nice on you."

Maybe you do have bags under your eyes, and you haven't lost all the extra weight you gained along with the last baby. It doesn't hurt to be honest; pull a little fat off your waist to see how good you'll look when you lose it, and give yourself a nice, positive little pep talk about going without supper tonight.

Resolve to go to bed as soon as the kids do for once. Mark it off as beauty sleep.

But never look at yourself—or think of yourself—without something positive to say! If you must be critical, immediately decide on some small positive corrective action you can take. Muse happily about the wonderful changes for the better you can choose to make for yourself. And make the most of what does look right, and what you have done right! That's being honest too.

You can depend on God to be positive in His feelings about you. Paul reminds us of this in a no-nonsense declaration.

> "If God is on our side, who is against us?
> He did not spare his own Son, but gave him
> up for us all; and with this gift how can
> he fail to lavish upon us all he has to give?
> . . . I am convinced that there is nothing
> . . . in all creation that can separate us
> from the love of God in Christ Jesus our Lord"
> (Rom 8:31-39).

After all, if God feels like that about you, that's plenty of reason to feel great about yourself!

What's in a Pretty Face?

One of my favorite professors in college was getting on in years. He had taught for so long that he had much of life's lessons boiled down to axioms and diagrams. One of his unforgettable quotes was "You get the face you deserve when you turn 40."

I understood him to mean that habitual expressions, whatever they tend to be, eventually imprint themselves in the look of the eyes and the lines of the face. What this had to do with the Life and Teachings of Christ course I was taking I'm not entirely sure, but the thought certainly stuck.

I like anything pretty, and I have a woman's interest in a pretty face. Occasionally I'll show my husband an advertisement picturing several women. "Which is prettier?" I'll ask. We regularly disagree on features, which keeps the game interesting. I still can't completely understand what he finds attractive. He has a thing about noses; a nose will make or break a face for him, while the shapes of noses don't bother me at all. But we almost always find ourselves agreeing when we discount a face "because it has something hard about it."

I find more and more, as I watch the faces that pass me in life, that I pay little notice to the actual shape of a nose or chin line or cheekbone. It's the spirit shining out of a face that attracts my attention.

It's hard to read the description of the bride in Solomon's Song of Songs without a bit of envy. No doubt this woman was physically pretty; Solomon's glowing descriptions of her lovely features left very few of them unmentioned. But one passage is especially striking.

> "Who is this that looks out like the dawn,
> beautiful as the moon, bright as the sun,
> majestic as the starry heavens?"
> (Song of Songs 6:10).

What a sense of presence this woman must have had. She must have had such a wholesome opinion of herself and the world around her and of God that not a wrinkle of discontent clouded her face, and her eyes could hold the serenity of the dawn.

This makes me stop and think when a particularly bitter thought makes my jaws clench and harden, and the skin around my eyes crinkle. Life hands out bumps and bruises, but do I want them to show on my face?

46

It's a funny thing—I've found that just loosening my jaw helps my thoughts run along gentler veins. Smiling helps me think happier thoughts. Singing helps, too. And good thoughts do better for my face than moisturizer.

After all, I do care about my face. Don't we all? We may not have the classic features of a model, but what we have we like to take care of and improve upon. And when all is said and done, though we can't control our physical features, we can control what is more important in the long run. We can control the attitude we nurture in our hearts, which in time becomes the spirit shining out of our faces.

Leaping Before the Lord

I can remember vividly one particular visit to the neighbors I made after our third baby was born. David, my husband, was home from college, a trip he made only once a month because it was so costly, and he was in the house with the children. It was the first time I had stepped outside without a child in my belly or on my back or hanging onto my hand in a very, very long time.

I felt half my normal size. I felt so light I could fly. It was a heady experience. I began to run down the hill.

I do know how to run. As a child I could run like the wind, and run half the day, too. As a teenager I ran in the empty halls at school, though it was against the rules, because I simply couldn't see that space stretching in front of me without running through it. I ran like a little kid to classes in college, while everyone else walked like grown-ups.

But now I was a mother, and I hadn't run in years. Though my head felt light and free, the rest of me had forgotten what freedom of movement was like. The bounce and spring in my legs was gone; I felt like a basketball gone flat.

I know all the arguments moms have about not getting enough exercise. My husband can recite them by heart, he has heard me explain them so often. There's the one about being too tired. After running around the house all day, bending over a thousand times to pick up toys and kids, pulling them (toys and kids) out from under the bed where they've gotten stuck, scrubbing up spills on the floor and on chair legs and the table base, packing a baby on our back as we do the housework, haven't we gotten enough exercise?

If we take the children on a walk, we have to go their pace, which is not much exercise. If we wait till the children are in bed, we don't want to take another step, much less think about *exercise*.

There are lots of good arguments for the benefits of exercise. Exercise gives you a healthier heart and a fit body, lowers cholesterol and helps you regulate your weight, helps you sleep better, have more stamina, relieves stress, and so on and so on. But all these arguments didn't move me much.

They are good reasons for fitness, and they are enough to get many people on the road to physical exercise. But the logic that "I needed" to do something, that it was "my duty" to exercise, just wasn't enough to push me into more tasks when I was already overwhelmed with everything I had to do.

Do you know what started me exercising? We put up some mirrors in the bedroom. I couldn't help noticing the way I looked! I came to the conclusion that I really, really *wanted* to look good! I lost a little weight, and I liked what I saw. I thought I could lose a little more and like what I saw better. I did a few exercises to improve my figure, and they worked. My husband could tell the difference. And better than any argument, clothes looked better on me.

And then early one morning, as I was hurrying across the dark, greasy pavement of a gas station to pay for gas, I broke into a run and found the spring was back in my legs again. Such exuberance filled me that I leaped to grab a piece out of the sky, and I let out such a screech that if it hadn't been a dark, early morning, someone surely would have seen me and carted me off to a white room somewhere!

You recall the story of how David, in his happiness to be bringing back the ark to Jerusalem, "leaped and capered" before the Lord, dancing "without restraint" (2 Samuel 6:14, 16). A special blessing seems to come with health and freedom of movement. A certain vitality, an exhilaration that finds its expression in movement, joy in life, and delight in God. David wasn't delighting in his body, he was delighting in God—but what a joy it was to express his happiness with freedom of movement.

One of the most thrilling verses in Psalms runs like this.
"The mountains skipped like rams,
       the hills like young sheep.
What was it, sea? Why did you run?
       Jordan, why did you turn back?
Why, mountains, did you skip like rams,
       and you, hills, like young sheep?
Dance, O earth, at the presence of the Lord,
       at the presence of the God of Jacob"
(Psalm 114:4-7).

If dancing and leaping in the presence of God seems a faraway experience for you, something your body is not quite up to yet, take courage. You'll be amazed at what small attempts at improving your body, often repeated, will do. Keep checking up on yourself in the mirror, and take lots of notice of every little improvement. These small rewards give you confidence and keep you going.

The exuberance that you feel when you are happy with the way you appear and feel is worth looking forward to and planning for. It's one of the joys of life that God designed you to have!

TOFM-4

49

Our Many Selves

In my closet hangs a forest-green velveteen dressing gown with peanut-butter fingerprints on the skirt and several small holes where it was scorched when I was trying to blow on the fire in the wood stove.

Beside it hangs a new dress with a sweetheart neck, blooming with large bouquets of bluebells, grape hyacinths, and pink poppies. I feel like a girl in that dress! But it's not the thing to wear when I'm teaching or giving a workshop at a convention, so I have skirts and blouses and sweaters that give my image some credibility when I need to look like I know something. And if you must know, there are also some satiny night things for a very private, delicious look.

In the clothes in my closet I find myself reflected in as many different images: confident and professional, sensuous and alluring, warm and nurturing, dusty and streaked, independent and free-wheeling. More than just roles, my clothes reflect different aspects of myself. Sometimes contented, sometimes fierce, sometimes capable, sometimes impossible.

My many different selves don't always coexist as tranquilly as the clothes in the closet, however. My mothering self feels guilty when my career self works overtime. After days of heavy mothering, my personal self feels edgy and restless, and I ache to shut out the world and read, walk, and think.

My career self longs for empty days in which to keep the house straight two or more days in a row. But after mopping up the same floor, washing the same dishes, and folding the same laundry over and over again, I find myself thinking wistfully of some job, any job, that once done stays done. Sometimes it seems that whatever I do, part of me is never satisfied.

It's important to take a good look at who we really are as women, and what we need to do with ourselves to fulfill God's plan for us. When there is war between the different aspects of our natures, it is often because legitimate parts of our selves are not being allowed expression. Pressures build up that can explode in uncomfortable ways.

It's important for us to come to a "sober estimate" of ourselves, as Paul advises in Romans 12:3. God has created us with vast capabilities that need to be understood and used if we are to be happy. In Corinthians, Paul describes how each of the body parts depends on the rest of the body in order to function. These comments can be applied to our mental and social selves, too.

> "God has combined the various parts of the body, giving special honour to the humbler parts, so that there might be no sense of division in the body, but that all its organs might feel the same concern for one another. If one organ suffers, they all suffer together. If one flourishes, they all rejoice together" (1 Corinthians 12:24-26).

Our various selves may jostle for their proper positions, but time and attention can help us find a healthy balance for all the different aspects of our natures. Not one of the many different parts of our nature could get along without the others.

For example, when the confident, professional me suffers a severe case of burnout, I find a lot of relief in doing the dishes. It's a job that's easy to do well, and no one is looking on to evaluate me! After a day of keeping up with everyone else's needs and feeling faceless, a touch of my husband's hand, a glance, a word, unveils a self that is good to look at and good to feel. It's a part of myself that I don't think I would have ever discovered on my own. Feeling good about my body and sexuality gives my more public selves a boost in confidence and vitality.

Try taking some time to look in your own closet. You might find some garments that reflect aspects of yourself that you ought to get rid of. You might find you are missing some clothing that would dress you for roles that are important for your own growth and development, or that will help you serve others.

Whatever you find, you can, with God's grace, create a closet of garments that reflects a whole you, the happy, fulfilled woman God designed you to be!

Juggling Dreams and Family

My sister gave me a small red-and-black book on zoology for my tenth birthday. The diagrams of how to make collections of skins and classify them intrigued me, and I decided to begin at once on a lifetime of animal study. I found a mousetrap and set it up in front of a hole under a gardenia bush.

A few days later I found a mole covered with ants in the trap. It was limp. Its eyes were gone. I could scarcely look at it or touch it, much less think about skinning it. That ended my career in zoology! But I didn't stop dreaming. I went on to explore other careers throughout my growing years.

As we grew to womanhood, most of us nursed a variety of ambitions based on our individual interests and abilities. Yet those of us who are also mothers are usually mothers by choice. We seek a full life, and that life for us includes being a wife and the mother of children.

The problem comes when we take on the responsibilities of a family and discover that our other options suddenly dwindle. In order to give our children the best start in life, many of us have stayed home. We find our hands more than full with child care. But our dreams don't die easily. We know we are capable of activities other than doing dishes and wiping little bottoms. We begin to feel trapped.

Fascinating fields of science, technology, business, and creative endeavors beckon us, even as we scrub the kitchen floor. We feel time whipping through our fingers like rope over the edge of a ship. The world is moving on without us, and we are afraid that our education will become outdated, that our special skills will slip. We are afraid that having a family means the end of the rest of our dreams.

Other people who try to help us find perspective say things like "Enjoy your children while they are small; they are little for so short a time." We smile and nod, for we know this is true, but we don't *feel* it is true. We feel like we have had children forever, and we will be sweeping up and picking up and wiping up after them for the rest of our lives.

"Your responsibility as a mother is so important," others say. "You shouldn't be hankering after other work." Yes, of course. Of course! We know this is true. But we still feel trapped, wondering whatever happened to the rest of our dreams.

Then God reaches down into our little fretting selves and says, "Bless the Lord anyway." Bless the Lord, indeed! Why?

> "Bless the Lord, my soul,
> and forget none of his
> benefits.
> He pardons all my guilt
> and heals all my
> suffering.
> He . . . surrounds me
> with constant love, with
> tender affection;
> he contents me with all
> good in the prime of
> life, and my youth is
> ever new like an eagle's"
> (Psalm 103:2-5).

You see, God makes Himself responsible for our contentment. We can depend on Him to make our dreams come true in His own time frame. That frees us to live without worry, surrounded with His love. What a reason to "bless the Lord, my soul."

Guilt and the Working Mother

Our generation of women is fortunate in some ways. We have more lifestyle options to choose from than our mothers and grandmothers. More and more mothers of very young children are going to work outside the home; in fact, they have been the fastest-growing segment of the work force since 1972.

Perhaps the romance of a career has caused part of the working mother trend. But a recent Congressional Budget Office report announces that couples with children have been steadily losing economic ground to the rest of the population. Many young mothers have had to go to work just to keep house and home together.

The slender line mothers have to tread between career and family is more like a teeter-totter than a balance beam. It is nearly impossible to keep the teeter-totter perfectly balanced between our family and work. And whichever end of the teeter-totter we find ourselves sliding down ends in a mire of guilt.

In our family the problem looks like this. We're a family of six living on one very part-time salary. If the only job that happens along is a full-time position for Mom (and a very nice one that will look gorgeous on her resumé—that's where the teeter-totter comes in), what's to be done? Well, there came a point where we decided I'd have to take the job. And that night I had a nightmare that cost me two years' growth. The memory of it still hangs on me like a horrible garment I can't shake off.

I dreamed that since I had to go to work the next day, I couldn't keep the children. In the middle of the night I drove to a large city several hours away and dropped them off near some homes with lighted-up windows. Still in my dream, I "awoke" the next morning and realized what I had done. I was swept with waves of anguish, guilt, and panic.

How could I ask the police to help me find the children I had abandoned? I knew that even if I ever found the street in daylight where I had left the children the night before, even if I found the *children*—who would let me have them back again? Who would believe that I was a fit mother?

Then I really woke up, shuddering and short of breath, and I could not believe I was awake and the children were really safe in their own beds. I felt that if the police even found out that I had dreamed such a dream, they would know I wasn't fit to have the children! After all, I felt I wasn't. I had decided to go to work full-time.

It's not my purpose to discuss here the pros and cons of mothers working; I just want to point out that it happens, and it leaves mothers in the throes of guilt. It would be nice to be able to pull out a Bible verse to assuage our guilt and give us peace when we have to leave the children and go to work. If we could do that, however, our comfort would be like a band-aid covering a deep sore that needs attentive care.

Guilt serves a purpose. It makes us concerned about a problem that might otherwise be too easy to ignore. But God does plan for us to go to Him with our guilt.

"Examine me, O God, and know my thoughts;
     test me, and understand my misgivings.
Watch lest I follow any path that grieves thee;

guide me in the ancient ways''
(Psalm 139:23, 24).

God gave us grave responsibilities when He gave us the care of children. I wonder, sometimes, how He ever dared to do it! He means for us to undertake the responsibilities faithfully, too. But His solutions to our needs are custom-fit; they are as varied as the problems we lay before Him.

We need to take time with God, and together come to an idea of what we should do. Then He can teach us to trust Him step by step, till we are wrapped in the warmth of His will, and guilt is the stranger out in the cold.

Adjustments

My sister's fiancé has announced that he is looking forward to having kids in the family, but he has a weak stomach as far as diapers and upchuck go. He really can't bear any of that kind of thing, he says, so she'll have to carry on through all of that without his help.

I'm not trying to pick on my sister's fiancé in particular, just husbands' expectations in general. Mine, for example, believes that vomiting should be practiced in the bathroom, preferably over the toilet. And I say that's all fine and good as long as he's willing to clean up the bed, the clothes, the throw rug, and the floor all the way into the bathroom after a sick baby has made the trip.

Many husbands are shocked at the upheaval children make in a household. They have a hard time understanding why babies make so much noise during the night and during the news program. They can't figure out why the daily schedule should suddenly have holes in it called ''naptime'' when the rest of the household is expected to muffle its breath and answer the phone before it rings.

"Children," these men proclaim, "should not interfere with the flow of life as it occurred before children made their appearance." This means that when Daddy is ready to make a trip to town to get groceries, it's time to go, even if the baby is sleeping. This means that travelers—even those in a Volkswagen Beetle—should not have to make an unscheduled stop just to change a baby's diaper.

Fathers, like mothers, have adjustments to make when children become part of the home. Fathers, however, unlike mothers, can take their own sweet time about it! That's where the rub comes in. One of the rubs, anyway. You probably can think of a few others from your own experiences!

The adjustments to a new way of life with children in the family creates tension in an already delicately balanced relationship between a man and a woman. Parts of our personalities show up that have never been evident before. Our husbands wonder whatever happened to the sweet, capable creatures they married. Whoever dreamed that the simple task of raising kids, which women have been engaged in since the beginning of time, could overwhelm them so completely? We wonder whatever happened to the men we were so sure would make wonderful fathers.

But all this new knowledge of ourselves, startling and often disappointing as it may be, is just another step on the road to understanding each other. The discovery of a weakness in yourself is humbling, but it's very useful when you meet up with a similar weakness in someone else. As you understand your own humanity more and more, you are in an excellent position to be more accepting of another's humanity.

Though our mates may no longer occupy the pedestal they did when we first married them, we don't end up smelling like perfect roses either. Love that can say "I see your good side and your bad side like I never saw them before, but I still choose to love you despite any mistakes you have made or will make" lends a warm security and depth to marriage. Love that knows and still loves is sweet and wonderfully easy to live with.

"As a father has compassion on his children,
so has the Lord compassion on all who fear him.
For he knows how we were made,
he knows full well that we are dust.
Man's days are like the grass;
he blossoms like the flowers of the field;
a wind passes over them, and they cease to be,
and their place knows them no more.
But the Lord's love never fails those who fear
him" (Psalm 103:13-17).

God's complete acceptance and love for us, though He knows every detail of our weaknesses and failures, gives us a chance to feel the wonderful peace that comes of being loved despite what we are. It also gives us a secure base from which we can love our mates without strings or expectations, through the stresses and strains of raising children.

Searching Again for Love

It's a bald fact that we wouldn't have become moms without sex. For some of us, however, that idea fails to make its full impact on our consciousness. Our husbands entertain the idea much more readily.

I remember when my pregnancy with Josh was in its first months. My husband told me teasingly, mimicking Bill Cosby, "I can hardly wait till you get big enough for me to point out to everyone that I did that!"

I was flabbergasted. Pending motherhood had so engrossed my attention that I had forgotten Dave had anything at all to do with my having a baby!

Becoming mothers gives a big jolt to our roles as wives. Because the demands of the mother-child relationship are so intense, our husbands are often bumped into second place in our priorities, though we may never consciously intend to place them there, and they certainly aren't happy there.

Even *we* don't completely understand why the babies take all our energy and emotions. We become exhausted and desperate taking care of them. But no one else, including the children's daddies, seem to be able to care for them as vigilantly as we do, and so we worry on.

In time, however, most of us begin to wonder if we really need to monitor every grimace and burp. Little by little we learn to relax our death-grip on our mothering responsibilities as we adjust to long-term motherhood. It's a long, uphill road, but eventually we learn to take deep breaths again, to stop and look at the flowers.

We begin to discover ourselves again. And somewhere along the way we discover our mates again. At least let's hope we do. Many couples become so absorbed in raising the children that they never do find each other again, and when the children leave home, their marriages flounder.

In rediscovering a mate, we usually find ourselves coming to terms with a tattered relationship. It's had to take care of itself for a while. The bloom and glow of romance takes a severe beating under the financial, physical, and emotional stresses of raising a family. We find that we have to make a decision to recommit ourselves to a relationship that has become ragged and unappealing.

My relationship with Dave suffered seriously in the demanding fog of child care. But I had decided to live with him for better or for worse, whether I liked it or not, and I figured life would be much better if I liked it! I determined to love him regardless of my feelings. It was a fortunate choice! God took me in hand, and taught me how to fall in love again.

In the poetry of the Song of Solomon, the bride describes her efforts to find her love.

> "Night after night on my bed
> I have sought my true love;
> I have sought him but not found him,
> I have called him but he has not answered. . . .
> The watchmen, going the rounds of the city, met me,
> and I asked, 'Have you seen my true love?'
> Scarcely had I left them behind me
> when I met my true love.
> I seized him and would not let him go
> until I had brought him to my mother's house,
> to the room of her who conceived me" (Song of Songs 3:1-4).

Do you need to find your true love again? You fell in love with him once, so you know it's possible! Reach out to him daily, hold him fast, and take the time to craft together the intimacy on which rests the happiness and security of a home.

Intimacy

Norman Rockwell did his work with such humanity and humor that it's easy to see ourselves in his story paintings. In his spring illustration for *The Four Seasons of Love,* a red-haired, straw-hatted boy beguiles his girlfriend with tunes from his flute, surrounded by loving pairs of wild friends.

In the summer painting, a young woman with sweet dreams

in her eyes and daisies in her lap is wooed by Mr. Dark and Handsome. Winter love is illustrated as the platonic relationship of a silver-haired gentleman and matron chatting over cups of coffee beside a dancing fire.

But my favorite painting is a picture of autumn's love. "It is what I call comfortable love," Rockwell said in the American weekly in which the pictures were first published. "Autumn depicts the era into which I am entering. Here is the time of love when she can sit with her hair in curlers and he wear his bedroom slippers, when they can understand the silences, when they don't *have* to talk. This is the love of adults who know each other well."

The plump middle-aged couple that sat for his painting were married to each other. Rockwell said that while they posed, the wife constantly interrupted the sitting to give her husband an affectionate pat and kiss, tickling Rockwell's sentimental soul!

I like autumn love because it speaks of intimacy. It speaks of a deep, penetrating knowledge of each other based not only on the experiences of everyday companionship, but on sharing crises, too. The good and bad experiences of everyday life, in big and small ways, bring to light the real person we married.

The passion and idealism of summer love have mellowed. Passion is still with us, but it's more warming and sustaining than wild and driving. It's still strong, but more directed and under control. Idealism matures with experience. It too becomes a more comfortable bedfellow, because it is couched in reality. We know better what we are, what we can achieve as individuals and together.

I like knowing my husband. I adored him when I married him, but I can't say I adore him now. I know him better, and he isn't everything I ever dreamed a man could be. But flesh and blood is a lot more fun than dreams! He's interesting and challenging. I'm fascinated with the way he thinks. His logic may be upsetting at times, but it's never boring.

I like being known by my husband, too. I wish he wouldn't

get angry when I cry. Crying is one of the things I do, and he can't relate to it. But he knew what I was thinking the other morning after a cold night in the woods. Heather announced that she froze the whole night. All my mothering instincts rose up in horror. Her sleeping bag was so thin.

"Didn't you cover her with that blanket and my down parka?" I asked my husband. He had. "But I decided to use that big coat for a pillow," Heather said. I looked at Dave a long time, and all the things I wanted to say but didn't know how didn't need to be said anymore.

Emotional intimacy and physical intimacy go hand in hand. Who can say which precedes the other? Because I am physically intimate with my husband, I can dare to show him an emotional vulnerability that doesn't intimidate him like my crying does. It still takes lots of courage to do it, though, because he still doesn't know me very well, and he still isn't very careful with my feelings.

I've had to grow a thicker skin in order to live with him. He calls it "independence" and doesn't care for it too much, but that's all right. It makes it possible for me to keep myself intact while I'm emotionally vulnerable, exposing myself to the roughness of his masculine nature in search for more knowledge of him.

Sometimes this means asking his opinion and trying to listen when I'm too happy—or too angry—to care what it is. Sometimes it means being mad and telling him exactly what I think, whether he wants to hear it or not. Sometimes it means swallowing my pride and being understanding when I'd rather be mad. Sometimes it means sounding—and looking—silly, risking his ungentle laughter in order to try something new in our relationship. Often it means looking at life from his perspective rather than from my own for a while. The road to becoming intimate isn't all satin and lace and quiet talks, but even the rough parts are worth traveling.

Intimacy with my husband has changed me. Since I married

him I feel much more attractive, confident, and—well, sexy! Many times a day he lets me know that he still finds me physically attractive, and I thrill with every assurance. You'd think I'd be used to his assurances after 10 years, but I'm not. He is proud of my accomplishments, though he never fails to note that I still can't put the ketchup bottle back in the same place twice.

One of the prettiest verses in the Song of Solomon goes like this.

"My beloved has gone down to his garden,
  to the beds where balsam grows,
to delight in the garden and to pick the lilies.
I am my beloved's, and my beloved is mine,
  he who delights in the lilies" (Song of Songs 6:2, 3).

Intimacy is a warm, beautiful part of married life, but it doesn't come with the license. It's a very personal treasure, both given and searched for, over and over again. It's like looking for the lilies in the garden of love. The more lilies you pick, the sweeter and more luxuriantly they grow, and the easier they are to find.

In the Valleys

It would be nice to think that after we marry, life only gets better and better. It's more realistic, though, to realize that there are hills and valleys in every journey. Sometimes the valleys may be very deep and take a long time in crossing.

Important things have happened to me in the valleys of our married relationship. I can remember one particularly dark time. I was in my ninth month of pregnancy with our third child. Dave had been struggling with unemployment for some time, and had only a part-time job.

His mood seemed to get blacker and blacker, and all I knew to do was stay quiet and out of his way. I didn't know it at the time, but he had been receiving threats to his person and to the security of our home. For three weeks he didn't speak to me except in the bitterest of terms.

During those terrible days I learned three things. I learned that I could still choose to love him in his blackest moments. I faced the possibility of having to live with a hostile man for the rest of my life, shuddered before it, and realized that if God asked me to do it, then it was possible.

Second, though I couldn't understand his deep despondency, I decided that I would refuse to let Dave or anyone else make my life miserable. Though his despair deeply affected me, I realized I could not run his life. But I still had control over my own attitude, and I could choose to be happy.

Finally, I realized that I could depend on no human being for security and love. Only God's love would never fail.

Those have been some of the most important lessons of my life, and I've never regretted them! They have anchored my emotional security. I do not fear what the future can do to me or Dave, for I know that my happiness remains in God's hands and my power to make choices.

Sometimes the valley in a relationship turns rocky and treacherous. Perhaps it shouldn't be called a valley anymore—a ravine would describe the situation better. The bottom seems to have fallen out of your relationship. Somewhere along the way, you discover you've fallen out of love.

It's frightening to own up to the fact that you don't love the man you're married to. But it's not the end of the world. It's all part of the journey.

There are more ties that hold a marriage together than just love, and many marriages exist with just those ties. But they aren't the happiest marriages. They aren't nearly as fun as a romantic, loving relationship.

If you're looking for a whole relationship, you might just have to decide to love an unlovable man! But there are certain things you can do to make the job easier. Sometimes what you need is more information about the man himself.

I realized I was out of touch with what had been happening in Dave's life. I didn't know about the threats, and I was only slightly familiar with the cultural pressures and tensions he was experiencing. Since Dave didn't offer this kind of information, I learned to question him about his experiences and feelings. This is a man who can hang up the phone with little recall of the conversation he just finished. Unloading information about his day isn't easy, but we work on it.

During those three black weeks, Dave had been struggling with a difficult question of whether to go to nursing school. He had decided that the only way to solve his unemployment problems was to get a nursing degree, leaving me alone during a bitter Montana winter with a new baby and two small children. Knowing my difficulties with life's details, he was sure none of us would survive.

When he finally broke his bitter silence to tell me about his decision, he said, "I know you'll die. You'll lock yourself and the children out of the house in the middle of a blizzard and lose your way down the hill when you go for help."

Nothing seemed insurmountable after those three weeks of no communication! It was a relief to know what the problems really were. I urged him to go to school.

I did manage to lock myself out of the house. I went out for wood one night after the older children were in bed asleep, and the stick securing the sliding-glass door fell into place behind me. The baby heard me at the children's window, and crawled to the bedroom doorway. Between her screams and my banging, we managed to wake 4-year-old Josh, who let me back in. I could mention a few other close calls, but suffice it to say we managed to survive, despite my husband's dim view of our chances!

You may have certain inalienable rights, but when you commit yourself to a relationship, you may need to to relinquish some of them for a time in order to advance the long-term happiness of you both.

You don't relinquish your individuality or principles that you hold. Neither of you could respect the other if you do that, and respect is the foundation of your relationship. But you may have needs that your husband cannot fill. Commitment may mean resigning yourself to a less than perfectly fulfilling life (what are the chances of that here on earth, anyway?) in order to be happy with what you do have together.

And that brings me to the fun part of falling in love again. In choosing a partner, you choose a one-of-a-kind. There never was, or never will be, anyone just like him. His thoughts, his hopes, and all the best parts of his nature are for you to discover and make the most of. It is your private privilege! It always helps to remember that you fell in love once. All the wonderful things you found before are still there.

Courtship tends to magnify all the good qualities of a loved one. Marriage tends to reverse that tendency, and we magnify the differences and problems we come across. But living with a man is much easier when you capitalize on his good points. It makes sense to look for the good.

One counselor advised saying thank you for 10 things every day. Having to say thank you to your partner makes you see nice parts about him you may never have noticed before.

Another idea is to look for a need your husband has, and secretly work to fulfill it. The more you look through his eyes, the more you try to make him happy, the easier it will be to fall in love with him again. Sometimes it's just a matter of forgetting yourself long enough to see your husband again.

Love is a decision. It's not the same thing as feeling in love. Tides of feelings come and go. Everything about living organisms seems to come and go in cycles. We can learn to be comfortable with our cycles, to understand the good part of having low tides as well as high tides in our feelings.

We can't control our feelings, but we can control the decisions we make and the things we do. Peter had an interesting piece of insight on how we learn to feel love.

"Now that by obedience to the truth you have purified your souls until you feel sincere affection towards your brother Christians, love one another whole-heartedly with all your strength" (1 Peter 1:22).

Acting the way you should as a way to learn to feel the way you should is a principle of human nature. We help children learn respect, reverence, courtesy, and a host of other attitudes that way. We can't require them to *feel* respect or reverence, but we can ask them to use certain words in addressing others, to walk quietly in the sanctuary, to *do* those things that nurture the attitudes we hope they will develop.

Feeling in love is a wonderful part of falling in love, but since what you feel is out of your control, don't worry about how you do or don't feel. Treasure your husband, and one day those feelings of love will surprise you, lighting again in your heart like an elusive butterfly that comes to rest when you aren't looking.

Always a Mother

My mother has followed every page of this manuscript with deep interest. My husband isn't sure if he wants to buy the book, but I know she will. She has kept my letters from way back when I was writing home from summer camp.

"How can you write this book, and take care of the children and the housekeeping and the cooking?" she wants to know.

"Why, I can't, Mother," I tell her. "Something always has to give—the book, or the housekeeping, or the children, or the cooking. Sometimes it's one thing, sometimes it's another."

She nods, with a worried look on her face. But she still wants to hear my latest piece of writing.

She made a scrapbook of her first grandchild for me, writing down pieces of my letters about his development from month to month, to go with the pictures. Her interest in her children is excelled only by her interest in her grandchildren. She sees them through a grandmother's eyes, which are keener than anyone else's in the world. She worries about their crooked little fingers, their haircuts, and whether they know enough math.

My mother's mother is like that too. Even at 91 she is a great letter writer, and she keeps up with her large extended family. She remembers everyone's birthdays, and takes great interest and joy in weddings and graduations.

Once a mother, always a mother, they say. Nana still keeps an eye out for her children's children's children. She walked by the kitchen one day, when Sarah was sitting up on the counter, helping us cook. "I just read somewhere that it's very dangerous to let your children sit up on the counter," she said.

And it was her sharp eyes that caught sight of the baby preparing for a headfirst tumble down the basement stairs, though the room was crowded with lots of younger moms and dads and aunts and uncles much closer to the staircase.

The children enjoy playing in her room, and she likes to have them. While we were taking a walk yesterday, she pointed out Angela, running around the yard in one of my skirts.

"She was in my room, wearing that skirt," Nana said. "She danced this way and that way, putting her foot up on this side and then her other foot up on that side. Then she got up on the couch and danced. She put her foot up"—Nana paused for effect—"and over the lamp went."

I gasped, and Nana laughed. "She looked so scared. I said, 'Let's see if the lamp is broken.' We tried it, and it still worked.

But," Nana went on, some concern in her voice, "Angela still looked scared. That was yesterday, and you know, she hasn't been back in my room since."

I'm happy to report that Angela has gotten over her fright, and today is playing in Nana's room again. "Go look at the children playing in Nana's room," Mother whispered to me. "They are so cute."

I did look, and I didn't see anything special. But there's no accounting for a grandmother's taste.

> "Can a woman forget the infant at her breast,
> or a loving mother the child of her womb?
> Even these forget, yet I will not forget you.
> Your walls are always before my eyes,
> I have engraved them on the palms of my hands"
> (Isaiah 49:15, 16).

How amazing God's love is! And there's no accounting for it, either.

Sisters

Mothers are never just mothers. We are usually daughters and wives and sisters and friends besides. These relationships add a marvelous dimension of experience to our lives. If having a brother is anything like having sisters, I've missed a lot. I wouldn't want to have missed having sisters for the world.

A sister is a mirror of what you are, and might be, but mostly what you are not. My sisters are taller than I am. Skinnier, too. They both have long, narrow, beautiful feet, and I don't. They can wear the kinds of clothes that look lovely on the models in the catalog books, but when *I* put them on, I look fat.

My sister Marcie has the brightest blue eyes. Mine are blue too, but not as blue as hers. When she looks at you and smiles, she half winks one eye. All the sparkles of blue come dancing straight into your eyes, and the effect is very charming.

My sister Linda is willowy and graceful, and her hands are magic. Whatever she touches turns into pure gold. If it doesn't, she knows where to go to buy something for $5 that will turn whatever she touches into something that looks like it's worth its weight in pure gold. Talk about beauty. Talk about taste. Talk about talent. And I haven't even mentioned wit.

My sisters can talk circles around me. I get so bewildered trying to follow what they're saying that I haven't the time to think of anything to say myself.

I have an insatiable curiosity as to what videos my sisters have seen and liked, what wallpaper they've put up, what new clothes they've bought, what new direction their careers are taking them. I don't like everything they like, but I like a lot of it.

When I do something to decorate my home, my husband usually doesn't have much of an opinion about it. First I wonder whether I like it or not. Then I wonder whether my sisters would like it or not. I use what I think their viewpoint might be as a sort of second judge in my head. It's a way of getting "our" opinion on a topic, rather than just juggling my own biases around.

I value what we three are together. We can talk about things we would never talk about to anyone else. We also get angry and hurt over things that wouldn't bother us nearly as much in a relationship with someone else. We worry about each other. We dream about each other when we're worried.

I fussed at my sister a few weeks ago. It was very poor timing; it was after her wedding, and I was helping her take her wedding dress off. I called her up later and apologized—not for the fuss, but for the timing.

"Why, Cheryl," she said, "you always say what you think,

and we still stay good sisters. Why should this time be any different?"

I sniffled and thanked her very humbly. It just shows you how good she is at being a sister. Let me quote a psalm, with a minor change; the original just says "brothers," but I'm sure it'll mean the same.

"How good it is and how pleasant
　　for brothers and sisters to live together!
It is fragrant as oil poured upon the head
　　and falling over the beard,
Aaron's beard, when the oil runs down
　　over the collar of his vestments.
It is like the dew of Hermon falling
　　upon the hills of Zion.
There the Lord bestows his blessing,
　　life for evermore" (Psalm 133).

The Proverbs Lady

In my college days I enjoyed researching the ideal woman. The lady in Proverbs 31 was one of my favorite people. My sister-roommate, taking advantage of this passion of mine, encouraged me to draw pictures about the Proverbs lady's activities. As a surprise, she machine-embroidered these sketches onto quilt blocks. My youngest sister machine-embroidered the verses that accompanied them onto other blocks. My mother worked on the project too, and together the three of them crafted a beautiful queen-sized quilt for a wedding present.

It was not long after becoming a bride and eager to prove

myself as a wife and mother, however, that I sustained a real shock. I couldn't believe that a small attic apartment with two occupants could be so impossible to keep clean.

I had never had any problem keeping my bedroom straight, but the job that faced me now was of entirely different proportions. It included picking up after an ex-bachelor who was used to his belongings lying out in the open where he could see each and every item.

I couldn't keep the bed made, either. My childhood habit of making it upon rising lasted for about three days after we moved into the apartment. I soon discovered that my new husband was of a humid composition. The bed actually had to dry out for several hours before it could be made, by which time I was long departed on other business.

Living in an apartment that was an embarrassment was an unhealthy evironment for my idealistic visions of what a wife should be. I tried very hard not to think of the Proverbs lady. When I became a mother, any thought of her brought on depression. I relegated the wedding quilt to the top shelf in the closet, ostensibly because it was too good to use, but really because it was too hard to look at.

After all, I reasoned, experience had taken me beyond the idealism of my girlhood and brought me up short against reality. The Proverbs lady far outclassed me. If she was the ideal woman, I wasn't even in the running. This woman was into banking, real estate, social work, and teaching, and she ran several businesses as manager and sole employee.

Despite her numerous careers that apparently ran concurrently, this woman's laundry (she was also a mother) was always done, and her meals were prompt and satisfying. "She rises while it is still night" (verse 15). She undoubtly found little use for bed at all. With this woman around, who needed a town council? She could handle everything.

And what woman common with the rest of humanity would admit that she doesn't give a fig about charm, and doesn't care about her looks—that all that matters are her achievements? I didn't think I wanted to meet someone like her.

I finally decided to come to terms with the Proverbs lady. I sat down and drew up a chart of what she was, and what I wasn't. After thoroughly studying the whole discouraging picture, I think I have come up with a few pieces of insight that make this wonder woman easier to take.

Perhaps she wasn't one woman at all! Perhaps Solomon was just trying to describe some of the many talents women have. As a whole, the verses actually put together a pretty liberal picture of women's abilities, compared to the low role many women played in society then—and sometimes even now. And despite the uncomfortable dig about charm and beauty, it is an unescapable fact that what we do is worth a lot more in the long run than what we look like and how we flutter our eyelashes.

Rather than a call to be a perfect superachiever, perhaps Solomon wanted to appeal to the noble, high-minded side of woman's nature. Perhaps he wanted us to see the magnitude of our possibilities in dignified, competent, virtuous industry. Perhaps, if I can see past my defensivness, I can recognize Solomon's generous intentions! And indeed, one of his descriptive passages sounds very attractive.

"Her sons with one accord call her happy;
her husband too, and he sings her praises:
'Many a woman shows how capable she is;
but you excel them all' " (verses 28, 29).

I still have ideals, but my goals as a woman take into account my weaknesses now. I don't expect to be more capable than any other woman, but it would be nice if my husband thought I was! I may not always be able to manage my career, laundry, and meal schedule in perfect synchrony, but through thick and thin I hope I can be the kind of woman my children call happy.

Solomon adds that "it is the God-fearing woman who is honoured" (verse 30). To be God-fearing is also a goal of mine.

And not an intimidating one, for with relief I realize that in a warm relationship with God, everything else good in my life is realized!

Quest for the Stream of Delights

Sabbath mornings are perhaps some of the most difficult hours of the week for mothers. I struggle with Angela's waist-length hair. "Who rinsed your hair last night?" I ask her. It's gummy, and I have to assume no one did. Heather can't find one of her shoes. It's stuck behind the shoe box rather than in it, but this takes 10 minutes to discover.

Angela slips on a wet front step and has a muddy streak up her white stocking. Sarah, also in white stockings, crawls across the floor of the car to retrieve a toy. The grime she picks up plus splatters of orange juice I missed wiping up on her dress makes her front more dingy than I feel appropriate for church, but it's still a shade better than everyday clothes.

After our hour-and-a-half trip to church, we all are considerably more disheveled than when we began. The back of Sarah's dress is still clean, though, and I gather what comfort I can from that. I hope church members who are appalled at the state of the front of her dress won't make an opinion on my mothering until they see how clean the back is.

It's a daunting struggle for young mothers to get everyone to church in a presentable condition and prepared for a few hours away from home. We pack sacks of clothing, extra underpants and diapers, stroller and blankets, storybooks, crayons and quiet toys, cups with covers, bibs, and food for potluck—but always seem to miss something. This week I realized I didn't have a needle and thread. Angela tore a visitor's dress, climbing on her lap.

Is attending church worth the trouble it takes? Perhaps it wouldn't be if all church meant was a run past the gauntlet of social approval! But there is more—much more—that keeps us coming and urges us to help our children discover the joy that attending church can be. The psalm writer puts it this way:

> "Gods and men seek refuge in the shadow of thy
>   wings.
> They are filled with the rich plenty of
> thy house, and thou givest them water from
> the flowing stream of thy delights; for with
> thee is the fountain of life, and in thy light
> we are bathed with light" (Psalm 36:7-9).

We come seeking the rich plenty of God's house! We want God's face to shine on us and on our children. We want to run splashing into the fountain of life and drink of the flowing stream of His delights, the water dripping from our hands and chins. He promises that we will be filled with His delights! And so we come with our children to His house, for we don't want to miss a drop.

Camp Meeting Oasis

The pastor in the lobby looked at the children kindly enough. "It's 8:00," he said. "My children have been in bed since 7:30. Don't you think your children should be in bed too?"

I couldn't argue with him, and so I marched the children out of the auditorium doors into the night. I could have told him that we had made preparations all day in order to attend the evening service. We had taken the day easy so that the children wouldn't be overtired, but had included enough new activities so they wouldn't end the day with restless boredom. I could have explained that the children had napped later than usual, and weren't sleepy. But I was too angry!

I wondered if his wife, at home with his children, ever wished she could attend the evening services. I wondered if he ever thought of how few services mothers of small children can attend, and when they do, how fragmented the messages are that they manage to hear. Perhaps it's hard for a pastor who attends so many services to imagine how hungry a young mother gets for preaching.

Moms often miss adult Sabbath school for years at a time, for by the time one child can attend Sabbath school alone, there is often a younger one who still needs mom's stabilizing influence. We can't get much more out of the 11:00 service, because it comes at the baby's naptime. Baby is not happy with her strained schedule, and the next oldest is still learning how to whisper.

Our personal devotions, too, have often suffered from the demands of the family. By the time camp meeting time rolls around, we are quite ready for a spiritual feed. But even at camp meeting it is not easy to find a few quiet hours to listen to God's messages, for children do not stop being children, even for the four days or so of camp meeting.

The psalmist knew what camp meeting is like. The Israelites often traveled to Jerusalem for religious services and feasts. He describes the deep emotions pilgrims have as we come to meet with God.

"O God, thou art my God, I seek thee early
  with a heart that thirsts for thee
  and a body wasted with longing for thee,
  like a dry and thirsty land that has no water.
  So longing, I come before thee in the sanctuary
  to look upon thy power and glory.
  Thy true love is better than life;

76

therefore I will sing thy praises. . . .
I am satisfied as with a rich and sumptuous feast
and wake the echoes with thy praise''
(Psalm 63:1-5).

Sometimes I feel self-conscious, slipping in and out of the meetings with children in tow, or sitting just outside a side auditorium entrance, my ear in a crack in the door as the children play around me. I am acutely aware that my children's restlessness can keep others from gaining their own camp meeting blessing, and I try to keep that from happening. But let me tell you this: The words I do manage to catch are treasures! They sink deep into my heart, ringing so true that tears spring to my eyes.

For you see, when we mothers long for God so deeply, and search for Him in His sanctuary, *we have God's word that we will be satisfied!*

Are We Having Fun Yet?

Every time I've come to church with a new baby, our resident bachelor, Tyler, scratches his head in amazement.

"You had to go get another baby?" he asks. "What's so great about having kids, anyway?" He's only half teasing, and he has a right to ask. He cleans up the floor after we have church potluck, and he can always tell where the kids ate.

His question always catches me off guard. "Why—well, you know," I stall.

But he really truly doesn't.

"Children are such a blessing," I say. "They are so much

77

fun.'' And just then one comes in screaming because she fell off the swing. Another one stalks in sulking because he has to sit on a chair until he can play more nicely. And finally we all catch a whiff of a full diaper as the toddler trots past.

"The behavior patterns I'm observing must be out of the ordinary,'' says Tyler. "They must be much different children at home.''

I swallow hard. "Well, no. . .'' I begin, but I can't seem to get much further. I think about his question all the way home from church and for days after. I like having kids, but I can't quite put my finger on the reason I do.

The joy of parenting is tied up with pain. It's hard to untangle the two. Children feel good to the touch. They are so huggable and kissable. But sometimes we get more touching and being needed than we bargained for.

Comments like "she's the spitting image of you'' and "he's got your gift of music'' stroke our sense of pride. But the other side of the coin is that our children also have our fits of temper, streaks of stubbornness, and crooked teeth.

For many parents the pain overrides the joy, and they learn to regret their decision to have children. One survey by Ann Landers asking the question "If you had it to do over, would you have children?'' was answered by a large majority of parents saying no. Perhaps the parents who would have said yes had my problem of figuring out *why*, and never got their surveys in the mail!

I decided to ask my father what he thinks is so great about having kids. He's had three, and we've been both a joy and a disappointment to him. In the past few weeks of vacationing at my folks' house, grandchildren have dripped apple juice all over the cream-colored carpet, creating stains that we haven't been able to get out yet. They broke one of the posters off the four-poster bed in the guest room. They lost a box of cartridges for his .22.

Heather, at the supper table, asked him, "Why are you so

interested in us, Grandpa?'' I noticed he couldn't answer her any better than I could Tyler. But I asked him again later, when he had time to reflect. And this is the gist of what he said.

Children are another outlet for our emotions. They are a source of companionship, different from that of a spouse. We desire something to give ourselves to, and so we have children.

Included in having children is the biological satisfaction of immortality. It's a somewhat selfish satisfaction, my father conceded, but we do face a little less fear of insignificance because a small part of ourselves will be left behind us.

Children bring with them the promise of growth. We love to watch them develop. There's always the element of surprise; what have we created? What will blossom forth unexpected, unfamiliar and unique, as a special mark of a child's individuality, a gift to the world?

Children bring hope. We hope that they will be receptacles of God's grace, and that because of them this old world will become a little happier, a little better off, a little more blessed.

This all brings to mind the question of why God made us in the first place. We have been a worry to Him, and more than just a disappointment. But those of His children who choose to return His love must be a multiplication of joy to Him.

You can hear the satisfaction in Eve's voice as she says, ''With the help of the Lord I have brought a man into being'' (Genesis 4:1). In each new baby is wrapped the wonder and potential of a new being. Each new baby of ours is so special it is as if it is the only baby in the world.

And when Jesus presents our children before His Father, they will still be wrapped in that garment of specialness. ''I am so glad you are Mine,'' the Father will say to each one. ''It's been wonderful having you as My child. Now I can have you close by My side, to enjoy for the rest of eternity. You make Me very happy!''

I wouldn't want to miss that day, would you?

A Time
to Be Angry

When I try to imagine God, I put myself in the middle of the universe. Space falls away beyond imagination below me, and reaches up to infinity above me. I see God's throne rising out of sight, its foundations in the bottomless fathoms. There are the thousands and thousands upon thousands and millions of angels in attendance to Him, and the rest of the countless numbers who are adoring Him. The very atmosphere thrills with the glory of His presence.

I put my small self right in the middle of all that, look God right in the eye, and try to imagine myself mad at Him. It's amazing, the dignity God confers on us. All His glory makes us look so insignificant that we ought to shrivel up into a tiny piece of dust and disappear into oblivion. But we don't. We stand right up there before Him as persons who get mad sometimes, as well as creatures who are filled with love and gratitude to Him.

What's even more amazing, God takes us seriously. He really wants to know what we think. He never lets the fact that He already knows what we think get in the way of our relationship with Him. "Come, tell Me," He says. And masks and cover-ups and happy faces just get in the way—you see how useless they all are when you look Him in the eye. He always gets right down to the real stuff.

I'm not saying it's easy to get mad at God. He takes from us only what's really truly honest: the bewilderment, the weeping, and just a little kicking. He accepts the truth from us, but not the self-pity, and definitely not any smashing-things-through-the-window.

"All right, now, buck up," He says. "What's really the matter?"

And I say, "I don't see how You're being fair, God. I know You are—don't get me wrong—but why on earth did You let this happen to me? How can You do this and call Yourself loving? (I can ask why once or twice, but any more than that God seems to count as mindless smashing-things-around.)

"You've usually been so good to me, God. And now I don't see Your goodness at all. There's just this big, black gulf, and You are nowhere in sight. You've disappeared and left me hanging in the middle of this pain, and I can't handle it. I don't know what to do with it.

"I'm really scared, God. I'm scared of *You*. I didn't think You would ever do anything like this to me. But there isn't anywhere else I can go for help—You're still my best bet. *I* certainly can't help myself out of this mess. So I'm depending on You to get me out of everything You've gotten me into."

I've learned to leave out most of the adjectives and adverbs like "never" and "unbearable" when I explain things to God. He usually goes through each one of them, making sure I meant exactly what I said. It's much easier to skip them all and be as straightforward as I can manage to be.

I've gotten so angry at God that the Psalms cut me to the heart like the love letters of a fickle sweetheart. I couldn't read them. I couldn't read sweet, loving promises. I couldn't read anything that praised God. Even the lamentations in the Psalms didn't contain strong enough language to say what I had to say to God, and I had to come up with my own words.

I like Job and Jeremiah and Moses, because they stood up to God and said what they thought. Being able to say exactly what is on your mind—no games, no insults, no clichés, just what's really there—is a wonderful part of intimacy. But God isn't above shocking us. He's into this intimacy bit, but He never lets us forget it's God we are being intimate with, that His thoughts and ways are as high above us as the heavens are above the earth.

Have you ever noticed how God responded to Job's arguments? He didn't even touch on what Job had argued about. It's as if God said, "Job, it's nice of you to take your time to talk about Me, but you know, you haven't the least idea who I am, really." Then God throws out these awesome descriptions for pages and pages, and finally Job gasps out, "I won't say another word—who can do justice by You?"

And God says, "You did just fine—don't worry about it. In your arguments and pain you sometimes lose sight of Me, and I thought you needed to see a little more of what I am. It'll help you."

Many times God doesn't answer our whys. He doesn't solve our problems. He just offers Himself. It's not that He doesn't have the answers—it's just that He knows what we need, and that's what He gives us.

> "Then Job answered the Lord:
> I know that thou canst do all things
> and that no purpose is beyond thee.
> But I have spoken of great things
> which I have not understood,
> things too wonderful for me to know.
> I knew of thee then only by report,
> but now I see thee with my own eyes.
> Therefore I melt away;
> I repent in dust and ashes" (Job 42:1-6).

God really has the nicest way of calming us down, and healing our anger!

Prayer

One morning when Dave was still away taking nursing, I found three puppies snuffling aimlessly about my back door. Their mother lived at the neighbor's, a half mile away. Apparently she had figured she'd had enough of them. Since I already had three puppy-things, she must have thought I wouldn't mind three more. Whatever her reasoning, I didn't agree with her! I had to get the puppies back where they belonged before they got too hungry or cold.

Since Dave had our only car, we were going to have to walk. I dressed the children in their snowsuits, piled the puppies into a box, and stuffed Angela in the backpack. I had all I could do to keep the puppies in the box and carry them, so I instructed Josh, 4, to hold Heather's hand. But that didn't last long. Two-year-old Heather had her own ideas of pace. As we marched along the shoulder of the highway, she began to fall farther and farther behind.

Our road doesn't get much traffic in the winter, but what it does get often goes fast. I heard a car coming up behind us on the other side of the road, and turned around to check on Heather. She was fine where she was, and I shouldn't have said anything; but since the shoulders on the road are so narrow, we make a practice of getting as far down the shoulder as we can, whatever side the car is coming on. I called to Heather to move away from the road.

Her baby brain must have been confused. The neighbor we usually visited lived in another direction, and we usually were on the other side of the road. She darted across the highway, straight for the speeding car. She was almost to the center line when she suddenly seemed to realize what she was doing, and ran back to our side of the highway.

The experience shook me. I could not walk back home with

the children along the highway, though once I delivered the puppies my hands were free to take care of Josh and Heather. We crossed snowy fields until we got to the highway, crossed it, and scaled a snow-covered cliff in order to get home.

I can hardly believe it myself, as I write this. The only place we were able to climb was 30 feet high, and half of it was nearly straight up and down. But a frantic mother can scale just about anything. I dug steps in the snow with my hands. I pushed the children up one step at a time by the seat of their pants, and I climbed up after them, with the baby on my back.

The cliff turned out to be much more dangerous than the highway. I nearly fell several times myself, because Angela's weight was pulling me backwards. And *then* what would have happened to the children?

We mothers tremble under the responsibility of the young lives in our care. They depend on us for their safety, health, and emotional and spiritual well-being. We agonize over the hitches in their social experiences. Will the problems they are having now create glitches in their social experiences for the rest of their lives?

The stubborn streaks. How can they go through life so resistant to input from others? Will they resist God, too? The disobedience. How can we help our children *want* to do right? Their crooked feet and teeth, too-big ears, knobby knees, weak eyes. We know only too well how cruel the world can be to what is less than perfect and beautiful.

Our anxieties make me think of what Jesus must have felt when He came to salvage what He could of this ravaged world. He could not live our lives for us. He could not reach out with a wand, zap us into purity, happiness, and health, and ship us off to heaven. That's what I would have wanted to do if I had been in His shoes. That's what I'd like to do for my children.

But Jesus didn't even zap His disciples, who were going to have to lead the church after He was gone, into perfection. We know that He drew power and wisdom for Himself and for others from prayer. One of His longest prayers recorded was for His 12 friends.

> "Holy Father, protect by the power of thy name those whom thou hast given me, that they may be one, as we are one." "I pray thee, not to take them out of the world, but to keep them from the evil one. They are strangers in the world, as I am. Consecrate them by the truth; thy word is truth" (John 17:11, 15-17).

We can't live our children's lives for them. We can't make them feel loving, respectful, ambitious, or brave. We can't make friends for them, make other children say nice things to them, make them get A's in school. We can't shield them from heartbreak and disaster.

But God has not left us to bring up our children without giving us everything we need to do the job. We need Him, and He has made His power available to us. We can plead for God's power to work in their lives because Christ spilled His blood for them. Before the Holy Spirit can do some of His most personal, private work, He waits for an invitation. But when we ask in Christ's name for these blessings, His Spirit can legally do work for our children He could not otherwise do.

Of course, He will not *force* the children's wills. And He doesn't always answer when and how we wish He would! But that is all very nice, because I, for one, would be terrified if I thought I could arrange my children's lives and direct God's actions. I wouldn't have the least idea what to do.

It is wonderful to know that we can talk on intimate terms to the God of the universe. He has all power at hand, He is on our side, and He loves our children! He has given, and will give, the best gifts of heaven for their eternal good.

It's Always Time
to Be Glad

If life could be compared to the sport of hot-air ballooning, I believe there would be two kinds of hot-air balloonists. The first kind would always have their heads in the clouds, and would find their contacts with the earth severely jolting and disappointing. The other kind would know earth intimately as mother. Their ambitions would begin with an aspiration to see above the grass.

I'm referring to the attitudes of optimism and pessimism. My first clue that people approached life with one or the other of these two attitudes came from my father. At one point in my childhood when I was trying to achieve a particularly daunting goal and he felt I would be disappointed, he told me a story that went like this.

"When I was a boy, I had an old rusty bike. Since we couldn't afford a new one, I determined to make mine look as new as I could. Entertaining visions of creating a smooth, enameled coat like what was on the new bikes I had seen, I sanded my bike down, painted it, and let it dry. The next morning I went out to the workshop to view my handiwork.

"In the hard, bright light of day, my bike looked nothing like I had hoped. The paint job was rough and knobby, and I was very disappointed. I just want to remind you that the end project never can quite match the picture in your head."

I looked at my father in amazement. It had never occurred to me that there were people who went around with bright hopes that were always being dashed. I never expect anything good to happen, and I'm almost always pleasantly surprised. Perhaps this is because pleasant surprises are the only kind of surprise I can stand.

I was in the car on the way to the hospital to have my fourth baby. It was one of those rare occasions in which I let down my optimistic mask, and show my true pessimistic nature. "Well," I said cheerfully to Dave, who was driving, "I hope you can manage all the children if I don't make it back."

Dave looked at me in shock. "You're not planning on making it back?" he asked.

"I *think* I'll make it through this childbirth," I explained. "But I don't want you to be surprised if I don't."

Dave looked at me like I had lost my mind, and I was reminded again that there are some people who don't look at life the same way I do.

"Look at that car coming toward us," I said. "Don't you ever think to yourself that this car may be the last thing we'll ever see? That this may be the car that hits us and kills us?"

My husband wasn't interested in the car. He kept staring at me.

My husband is one of those who has his head in the clouds and keeps bumping uncomfortably into reality. I'm one of the realities he can't get used to bumping into. He thinks I'm the one who has my head in the clouds. He prides himself on being a "realist." But he always thinks things are going to end up better than they do, and I'm the one who's never disappointed!

Hot-air balloonists who always have their heads in the clouds have to keep weighing themselves down so they won't rise clear out of sight. They have to keep reminding themselves and everyone else of the negative side of life in order to keep in contact with what's down here, but they are still surprised when bad things happen.

Those of us who have a hard time keeping our heads above the grass keep turning up the burner, working up more hot air all the time, in order to float at all. We keep talking about the bright side of life. That's why you hear people who are really optimists sounding like pessimists, and people who are pessimists, like me, sounding like optimists.

It's people like me who like Pollyanna. I first saw the movie *Pollyanna* when I was in academy, and for months afterward I wore lots of flamboyant ribbons like Pollyanna's in my hair. I like her philosophy, too. The one optimists look down their noses at, and call Pollyannish, because they have the idea that people who always talk about the bright side of life are ignoring reality. Optimists have to keep reminding themselves about reality, or else they'd forget all about it.

But they don't need to worry about us pessimists that way! We have our feet very firmly rooted in the facts of life. Pollyanna did in the story. She was an orphan, ensconced in a grim old house with little that was sympathetic to a little girl, and she wasn't likely to forget it. She just chose not to get stuck on the grim realities of life. She decided to be glad for the bright ones instead.

Paul advises a similar attitude.

"Be always joyful; pray continually; give thanks whatever happens; for this is what God in Christ wills for you" (1 Thessalonians 5:16-18).

Gratitude does wonderful things for us. It sends tides of healthful hormones coursing through our bodies. It lifts our emotions up on heavenly currents, and brings us almost within sight and sound of heavenly joys. When we learn to find God's hand and goodness in everything, when we can trust Him under every circumstance and thank Him for everything that happens to us, we begin to breathe the atmosphere of heaven.

We begin to understand a different reality from that of this earth. It's God's kind of reality, the real thing. It's what both optimists and pessimists need to feel relaxed and home at last!

We Shall Be
Led Forth in Peace

Both my grandmothers lost a child in infancy. In just about every story about the earlier days of our country, I've read of babies women lost. I've read of epidemics that swept through communities, taking two or three children in a family at a time.

At first, in my naiveté, I thought that since these women must have known the odds against raising a family intact, they would have taken the inevitable losses philosophically. But as I read more and more and had children myself, I began to understand that they were women, even back then.

Birth control has never been easy, but years ago it was practically nonexistent. You can understand how a woman with seven children would not be too happy over an eighth pregnancy, at least at the beginning. But when that woman's baby was stillborn, she grieved deeply, blaming the baby's death on her negative attitude during the first months of her pregnancy. Grief and guilt touched every member of that family.

Another moving story described a mother who mourned the loss of her first child so intensely she could not allow herself to love her second child. She was too afraid to love again.

Laura Ingalls Wilder lost a child. I often wondered why she didn't write more of her married life, until I learned that she couldn't bear to write about her loss. I've read of marriages that fell apart because parents couldn't handle their grief.

I'm not saying that sorrow doesn't touch our homes now. It surely does. But I'm staggered at the thought of how much more death faced earlier generations of mothers. And how the losses affected the surviving. Nearly every home in past generations was touched with crippling disease and loss, many of them tragedies that we don't have to worry about today, because of advances in modern medicine.

I know I have my family doctor and many others of his profession to thank for this. It's been a costly advance. But what mind-benumbing, heartrending grief they have saved so many mothers from experiencing. What gratitude springs up in my heart when I think of the lifesaving knowledge and skills my doctor has, and with what personal sacrifice on his part he has made medical care accessible to me.

I think about the other tragedies that for one reason or another haven't happened to my family yet. Car accidents, fires, earthquakes, famine. No one has fallen off the loft. When the baby fell off the stairs, she landed in an armchair. No one's broken an arm or leg. No one's even had to have stitches.

Along the highway I saw a billboard for health insurance, with the caption "The Accidents Waiting to Happen Have Already Been Paid For." I just wonder what the accidents are going to be. If I step more softly and look around all the corners, will I be able to prevent them?

This makes me think of the story of the old woman who was finally persuaded against her better judgment to take an airplane ride. At the end of the ride, when the airplane pilot congratulated her on her safe arrival, she said, "Well, you needn't sound so smart, young man. You might as well know I didn't put my whole weight down on that seat the entire time we was up in the air."

I guess I'm as silly as that old woman, thinking I can divert disaster by worrying about it. I know it's God's hand that has covered me and mine. There is no other explanation. But sometimes I wonder when His hand will quit covering us, and we too will have a tragedy.

Can I really thank God for His watchcare when so many others have been hurt in accidents, fires, earthquakes, and famines? It sounds almost like gloating.

I've thought a lot about this, my pessimistic nature being

90

what it is! I'll tell you what I've concluded, and I'll tell you why. We *can* thank God wholeheartedly for taking care of us. We can be glad we've escaped disasters others haven't. Any good that wins over evil is a triumph for God! We can rejoice over every one of God's triumphs.

The nature of the controversy of good versus evil being what it is, God won't wield His great stick and triumph everywhere just yet. But He will eventually.

> "I alone know my purpose for you, says the
> Lord: prosperity and not misfortune, and a long
> line of children after you" (Jeremiah 29:11).
> "For as the heavens are higher than the earth,
> so are my ways higher than your ways
> and my thoughts than you thoughts;
> and as the rain and the snow
> come down from heaven
> and do not return until they have
> watered the earth,
> making it blossom and bear fruit,
> and give seed for sowing and bread to eat,
> so shall the word which comes
> from my mouth prevail;
> it shall not return to me fruitless
> without accomplishing my purpose
> or succeeding in the task I gave it.
> You shall indeed go out with joy
> and be led forth in peace" (Isaiah 55:9-12).

I hardly know where to stop quoting from Isaiah. The way God talks of evil in the book makes us shudder with His powerful hatred of it. He has to show us the terrible consequences of living our lives without Him. The controversy of good and evil must be won fairly, on the basis of our choice for Him or against Him.

But however strongly he warns us, He never leaves us shuddering; He can't ever go long without showing us His longing to do good for us, to make the deserts burst into bloom, to bring us, shining with joy and gladness, into His glorious home.

In the bigness of God's nature, He hates evil and trouble even more than we do. The longer we walk with our hand in God's, the easier it is to be confident in His good intentions for us. We don't need to cower before the accidents that are waiting to happen.

Misfortune may come, but it's not God's *purpose* for us. It's only temporary. It may seem to fill our lives for the moment, but the moment will pass; it will never be the whole story. God's purpose us for *will* be accomplished. It is the triumph of God's glorious purpose that will be the story of the ages!

To Each Her Gift

After a long day working over the last pages of this manuscript, I happened to pick up a wonderful little book written by a man of prayer. I always start reading a new book in the middle. I can hear what a person is saying better when I jump right into the middle, and if I like it, I don't mind wading through any kind of beginning.

I was hooked in just a couple paragraphs. The man was talking about intercessory prayer, and he knew a lot about it. I practice intercessory prayer myself, but he was much more gifted at it than I am.

It was a wonderful book! Just a few pages of it gave me many new ideas. I resolved to be much more consistent and thoughtful in my prayers. But I couldn't help noticing that this man's faith was different than mine. It seemed to be stronger. He asked God for things that had never crossed my mind to ask for.

Was something the matter with *my* experience, that it was so different from his? I deal a lot with trust and faith in this book, but I come at it from such a different angle. It is a glorious thing to pray for God to turn a person's life around, and watch it happen before your very eyes. It seems a small thing to ask God to help me get the dishes done.

How self-centered our worries about our little homes can be—our little bit of dishes, a fussy baby, the spots on the rug. I began to wonder if perhaps what I was writing wasn't as important as I had thought it was.

After all, the world is fast spinning toward a terrible climax. Earthquakes are becoming stronger and more treacherous. The foundations of our economy are crumbling away, and it's only a matter of time till the whole structure crashes. Jesus is coming for us soon. Shouldn't I be writing about BIG things? Should I be writing about the same silly homely problems that happen over and over again?

Sometimes we moms get disheartened about the smallness of our work. That's not to say we don't get more exhausted doing it than the best of the great teachers and preachers in their work. And we know that growing children is a wonderfully worthy task. In directing our children, we may be staking out huge consequences in the world's history, years after our time. But we don't see the consequences now. And we do the same things over and over again. The sphere of our influence feels so small, everyday, ordinary.

In this book we've talked about the small, everyday, ordinary life so many of us live. It's helped me a lot in my own everyday life to be able to touch on the sore parts of our work, to laugh at our predicaments, to rejoice in God, our strong defender. The ministries of our lives may seem like small gifts compared to other gifts at first, but then we remember Paul's sage comment: "Suppose the foot should say, 'Because I am not a hand, I do not belong to the body' " (1 Corinthians 12:15).

It's a wonderful relief to realize that you or I don't have to be the whole body all by ourselves! Our gifts have their places in the work of God just as does the faith of the man of God who wrote that wonderful book on prayer.

"There are varieties of gifts, but the same Spirit.
There are varieties of service, but the same Lord.
There are many forms of work, but all of them,
in all men, are the work of the same God. In each of us the Spirit is manifested in one particular way, for some useful purpose" (1 Corinthians 12:4-7).

Each one of us mothers has a job only we can do. And God has formed us in such a way that His gifts make us especially happy when we use them.

Your faith is different from mine, and we can both be glad about that! Your unique position in this world gives you a unique view of what God is like. Your work, too, is different and special.

You can feel good about how God has formed you, and for what purpose you were created. We all need you, just the way you are!

Other helpful books for mothers

The Compleat Parent, by Nancy Van Pelt. This book offers easy-to-use methods of effective communication with and discipline for children of all ages. Paper, 156 pages. US$9.50, Cdn$11.90.

The Compleat Parent Workbook, by Nancy Van Pelt. Designed as a companion to *The Compleat Parent,* this workbook provides ways for parents to evaluate themselves and their relationships with their children. Paper, 76 pages. US$5.95, Cdn$7.45.

Kids: How You Shape Their Lives, by Ruth Jaeger Buntain. Drawing from 27 years' experience as a teacher, the author gives practical counsel on child rearing, with emphasis on imparting emotional and spiritual strength to the child. Paper, 78 pages. US$6.50, Cdn$8.10.

The Making of a Mother, by Karen Spruill. In this personal and surprisingly honest book, the author shares the discoveries that set her free from feelings of loneliness, frustration, and inadequacy. She also offers practical advice on breast feeding, toilet training, money matters, self-forgiveness, and discipline. Paper, 128 pages. US$7.95, Cdn$9.95.

Ask your bookseller or order from ABC Mailing Service, P.O. Box 1119, Hagerstown, MD 21741. Send check or money order. Enclose applicable sales tax and 15 percent (minimum US$2.50) for postage and handling. Prices and availability subject to change without notice.